Praise for *Street-Smart* ⅃

"Even people with good judgment and deeply rooted ethics sometimes find themselves in an ethical mess, often of their own making. In this readable book, full of real-world problems, Clinton McLemore guides us away from ethical messes, and out of them if we're in them."

—James A. Thomson, President and Chief Executive Officer, RAND

"Clinton McLemore defines a path that could lead to renewed confidence in the morality and responsibility of corporate leaders. This book should be required reading for those who venture into the world of business."

—Tony Campolo, Professor Emeritus, Eastern University,
author of *Revolution and Renewal* and *Let Me Tell You a Story*

"This is a book that should be read by CEOs, CFOs, anyone aspiring to be a senior business executive or, in fact, anyone who wants to make ethical decisions in the complex gray areas where we function in daily living. There is no reason that a commitment to strong ethics needs to conflict with success in life. Clinton McLemore is a long-time friend and adviser to me. His counsel has helped guide me in both my business and personal life. This book is a wonderful compilation of his knowledge and insight that should be helpful to anyone."

—Willis B. Wood Jr., Chairman, American Automobile Association (AAA),
Chairman and Chief Executive Officer (retired), Pacific Enterprises

"A great virtue of this book is that it provides solid grounding in basic business ethics, but also provides tools for resolving complex ethical dilemmas. I have known Clinton McLemore for almost two decades and trust his advice and counsel. He lives by what he teaches in this book, which is not something I can say about all management consultants."

—Debra Reed, President and Chief Financial Officer,
San Diego Gas & Electric and Southern California Gas Company

"*Street-Smart Ethics* is an urgent, practical remedy to heal the collective soul of American business, allowing it to hear the higher voice that breathed life into the greatest economic creation of humankind. The book shines proverbial light through the tunnel of business life and, to paraphrase Goethe, strengthens diminished talents best nurtured in solitude, so that the character of a nation can be best formed in its journey through the stormy billows of the new millennium."

—Jessie J. Knight Jr., President and Chief Executive Officer,
San Diego Regional Chamber of Commerce

"McLemore's book offers the reader timely and relevant meditations on life and our relationship to it. He has crafted a simple yet profound tool that offers help to anyone interested in the enrichment of his or her personal and professional life. I found it a thought-provoking and rewarding read. I've made it a member of my select 'Desk-Set' of books, and it helps provide a comforting sense of grounding in these turbulent times. . . . *Street-Smart Ethics* will provide a ROIC that will make any investor smile—and think."

—Charles Stott, Group Vice President, Raytheon Commercial Electronics

"Apart from its many insights, what makes this book such an interesting read is McLemore's masterful way of presenting actual cases. His development of ethical guidelines by using the Hebrew book of Proverbs is especially creative, a reminder that serious work in ethics is often more art than science. This book will be especially useful to people in the business world."

—J. Philip Wogaman, former Senior Pastor of Foundry United
Methodist Church in Washington, D.C., Professor Emeritus
of Christian Ethics at Wesley Theological Seminary, author
of *From the Eye of the Storm: A Pastor to the President
Speaks Out* and *Christian Ethics: A Historical Introduction*

"Writing with intelligence, humility, and optimism, Clinton McLemore has created an invaluable business and personal resource. By offering a broad view of ethical conduct and misconduct, this work drives home what it takes to treat others with dignity, honesty, and respect, even in the most difficult of circumstances."

—Joyce Rowland, Senior Vice President of Human Resources
and Chief Ethics Officer, Sempra Energy

Street-Smart Ethics

Street-Smart Ethics

Succeeding in Business without Selling Your Soul

CLINTON W. McLEMORE

Westminster John Knox Press
LOUISVILLE • LONDON

Book design by Sharon Adams
Cover design by Eric Walljasper

First edition
Published by Westminster John Knox Press
Louisville, Kentucky

This book is printed on acid-free paper that meets the American National Standards Institute Z39.48 standard. ∞

PRINTED IN THE UNITED STATES OF AMERICA

03 04 05 06 07 08 09 10 11 12 — 10 9 8 7 6 5 4 3 2 1

Library of Congress Cataloging-in-Publication Data

McLemore, Clinton W., 1946–
    Street-smart ethics : Succeeding in business without selling your soul / by Clinton W. McLemore.
        p. cm.
    ISBN 0-664-22628-0 (alk. paper)
    1. Business ethics.   2. Professional ethics.   3. Religion and ethics.   I. Title.

HF5387.M432   2002
174—dc21   2002028890

To Anna—

President of the Laguna Chapter of the National Charity League,
Gifted Leader, World-Class Mother, and Wife Extraordinaire

[The temptation to engage in unethical conduct] will come . . . in no very dramatic [way]. Over a drink or a cup of coffee, disguised as a triviality and sandwiched between two jokes, from the lips of a man, or a woman, whom you have recently been getting to know rather better and whom you hope to know better still . . . It will be the hint of something [that violates] the technical rules of fair play . . . something which the . . . ignorant, romantic public would never understand . . . but something, says your new friend, which "we"—and at the word "we" you try not to blush for sheer pleasure—something "we always do." And you will be drawn in, if you are drawn in, not by desire for gain or ease, but simply because at that moment, when the cup was so near your lips, you [could not] bear to be thrust back again into the cold outer world. . . . It may end in a crash, a scandal, and [a prison sentence]; it may end in millions, a [grand title], and giving the prizes at your old school. But you will be a scoundrel.

—C. S. Lewis

Contents

PART III. Testing Your Mettle

Acknowledgments

Writing about ethics inevitably brings to mind people in one's life who, in one way or another, have demonstrated excellence of character, in some cases by a singularly noble act that put them at risk and, in others, by the overall quality of their lives. This is my list of such persons: John G. Blanche, Robert L. Dallape, Frederick E. John, Nancie L. Mitchell, Mark C. Pocino, G. Joyce Rowland, and Anne S. Smith. My greatest admiration and appreciation goes to Willis B. Wood, who for many years, as CEO of a major corporation, showed many thousands of people what ethical leadership actually looks like in the flesh.

The following people have also demonstrated special goodness, and it gives me pleasure to honor them here: Hassina Albukhary, Daniel J. Alfonzo, Larry E. Andrews, Jeffrey S. Berryhill, Douglas D. Beyer, Bradley A. Brandmeier, David W. Brokaw, Warren S. Brown, Paul J. Cardenas, Dorothy A. Curiel, Carol L. Daderian, Dan I. Drane, Peter D. Esser, Mike P. Faberez, Robin A. Ferracone, Diana L. Firestone, Edward Fong, Kenneth E. Fosdick, William H. Freemel, Maye I. Fukumoto, Carolyn L. Fung, Lillian Gorman Frank, Daniel F. Gifford, Patricia L. Gimbel, Dana C. Gourley, James W. Gourley, Bradley J. Hallem, John R. Harbison, Thomas J. Herbert, Jon B. Hertzog, Bertha Jacklitch, Adam P. Jackson, Marion K. Jacobs, Richard R. Kilburg, David Kresge, J. Bret Lane, Claudia A. Lyons, Lawrence E. Mantle, Timothy A. Mefford, Anne M. Miller, Steven W. Miller, J. Trevor Milliron, Warren I. Mitchell, Rick M. Morrow, Michael F. Neiggemann, Eric B. Nelson, C. Richard Neu, Christopher B. Osborn, M. Scott Peck, Julian Popescu, Roy M. Rawlings, Roy R. Redenbaugh, Debra L. Reed, Charles B. Rooney, Alyn S. Rumbold,

David I. Sarkaria, Lee M. Stewart, Jaynie M. Studenmund, Patricia H. Summers, Barbara E. Schwartz, James A. Thomson, Karen Gardela Treverton, Dorothy Villasenor, Daisy E. M. Vollrath, James R. Ukropia, Donn E. Williams, and Iliana Zuniga (who was also helpful in pointing me to news articles relevant to the contents of this book). I express special appreciation to my son, Gregory C. McLemore, entrepreneur supreme, for encouraging me to become, once again, a person of letters.

Three people with especially fine minds assisted me, at one point or another in life, in further sharpening my own. I cite them here with profound appreciation: William V. Devlin, who used to drag me off to Fordham University to listen to Anthony Marra and who first taught me to think philosophically; Paul W. Sharkey, who, during the years that we served on the same faculty, pressed me relentlessly to justify nearly everything I said; and, the late Geddes McGregor, an Oxford-educated, erudite, and polymathic Scot whom I met one balmy summer day in my twenties when I was teaching at the University of Southern California. Not long after that, he became professor emeritus at that institution and we began to spend Saturdays talking about all sorts of things, from philology to psychoanalysis. I recall him saying that the claim to be "self-educated" was ultimately unsustainable, since we all learn from others, whether through lectures, articles, books, or tutorials. Those many Saturdays were, if anything, tutorials of the highest order, and I wish I could relive them. As exemplars of virtue, these persons have augmented my interest and enhanced my expertise in philosophical reflection.

Diogenes of Sinope (ca. 412–323 B.C.) is reported to have wandered about, lantern in hand, searching for an honest man. Writers, too, engage in a search, only theirs is for the perfect editor—intelligent, enthusiastic, supportive, unflappable, and wise. I have discovered such an editor in David M. Dobson, whose professionalism is unexcelled. He captured the vision for this book right off and helped to transform it, with lightning speed, into a reality.

Daniel L. Braden, the book's production editor, was also a delight; his luminescent mind, flawless attention to detail, and inveterate passion for fine book-crafting were sources of joy.

Robert W. Wentworth, through his continued enthusiasm for one of my earlier books, was the immediate impetus to the writing of this one.

The following persons commented constructively on one or another section of the manuscript: Robert D. Cadish, Edward Fong, and Paul W. Sharkey. And, Randall B. Peterson graciously took time to educate me about ethics in accounting. Whatever inadequacies remain in the text are completely my own.

Finally, I wish to express appreciation to my highly talented and consummately literate daughter, Anna-Marie, for her astute and helpful attention to the manuscript.

                                                                    C.W.M.

Introduction

L ife is filled with exciting and mind-boggling challenges, especially ethical ones. These challenges should be approached humbly but, at the same time, with a certain exhilaration and sophistication. This sophistication does not come from memorizing facts, learning to dazzle people with five-dollar words, or even reading the abstract works of eminent thinkers—although such reading can sometimes help. It comes mostly from being on the front lines, engaging with the complexities of everyday human existence, reflecting on what matters most in life, and caring enough to find out what others before you have considered important, and why. Our existence, if it is anything, is an adventure.

This is not a watered-down book filled with fluff or casual anecdotes. There are already enough books like that to fill the *Queen Mary*, including a number purporting to teach readers about ethics. It is a book that, I hope, will stimulate your thinking. While I make no attempt to offer legal advice in these pages, and precious little in the way of philosophical advice either, I think you will enjoy grappling with the issues and problems that I have laid out. Having worked as an organizational psychologist for almost two decades with some of the world's premier companies, I know how exciting work can be. I also know that it can be stressful. One purpose of this book is to help reduce whatever stresses you may feel when you confront ethical problems.

The term *ethics*, which can be traced back to Aristotle's *Nicomachean Ethics*, is based on the Greek word *ethos*. Similarly, the term *morality* can be traced back to the Latin word *mores*. Both mean having to do with habits, customs, and behavior. Today we usually use *ethics* to mean "relating to goodness" or, perhaps more exactingly, "rules, standards, or principles of goodness."

It is not easy to survive, much less thrive, in many modern business environments. The success of for-profit enterprises usually depends on winning, on beating out the competition, and this sometimes puts pressures on us that would have made a gladiator wince. It is impossible to cooperate and compete at the same time, which means that, when you get right down to it and have to choose, you cannot work simultaneously for and against the interests of another person or enterprise. We must constantly choose which of the two to do, and in what measure. As a result, real-world ethical decisions can test the mettle of the best of us.

The ethical problems we face, if not every day then frequently, often compel us to pit one obligation against another, the interests of X against those of Y, and sometimes to make compromises between competing but equally compelling duties. An ever-present challenge in life, for example, lies in finding ways to take care of others (individuals, groups, institutions, or society) without, at the same time, unduly injuring our loved ones or ourselves. The hard part comes when we must decide what, precisely, the term *unduly* means in the last sentence (not to mention "taking care of"). It may signify one thing to an unmarried soldier but quite another to a mother with small children. While we may not always be able to "do no harm," most of us want to minimize whatever harm we do. The question becomes how, precisely, to achieve this, especially when there are multiple possible harms, at least one of which *must* be done.

This book is divided into three parts. The first is a relatively short and, I hope, action-packed primer on ethics. It begins with an analysis of the much-publicized case of Enron. Prior to discoveries relating to WorldCom in the spring of 2002, the massive economic deflation of Enron Corporation sent shockwaves through financial markets around the globe. Its dramatic loss in value ("capitalization") was, at the time, the largest failure in the annals of American business, a loss that was more than doubled by the later devaluation of WorldCom.

I emphasize at the outset that everything in this book relating to Arthur Andersen LLP, Enron Corporation, Global Crossing, and WorldCom—or for that matter, any other company—is based on information presented in the public record, specifically in the news media. While little ambiguity remains about the financial status of Enron, Global Crossing, or WorldCom—all one need do is look up their respective stock prices—the nature and extent of culpability, if any, on the part of these or any other company mentioned in this book, or of any individual connected with them, remains to be determined.

After identifying the more salient ethical issues to emerge from these case studies, we will move on to these important topics: the relationship between law and ethics; choices open to us in the face of pressures to behave unethically; simple versus complex ethical dilemmas and the nature of "tragic moral choices"; how ethical problems may usefully be viewed through the lenses of a personal liability suit, specifically of a kind of malpractice; the psychological processes that sometimes accompany ethical-legal infractions; and, very briefly, the two major ways in which some of the world's greatest thinkers have approached normative ethics. I will also present some practical tools for ethical decision making. These will not always tell you exactly what to do when you face some of the more complex ethical trade-offs discussed in Part I, but they should sensitize you to the kinds of ethical subtleties you may encounter in your work.

The second part of *Street-Smart Ethics* is different in both tone and content. Presenting fifty guidelines based on one of civilization's most impressive works of literature (the book of Proverbs), it emphasizes the value of simple prudence. Among the best ways I know of staying out of trouble is to avoid situations that, by nature, seem to breed it. I discussed all but one of these proverbs in an earlier book, *Good Guys Finish First,* and have included them here because, in my judgment, they were just too valuable to leave out. Although I have revised and updated this material, the core message of these "wise sayings" has not changed in thousands of years: *Steer clear of trouble by spotting it well in advance and by acting honorably, conscientiously, and nobly.* This, I contend, is the essence of being "street-smart" in the best sense of the term.

In the third and final part of the book, I present a set of objective questions that will allow you to evaluate your sensitivity to ethical issues. I have also included eight ethical brainteasers that I believe you will enjoy and perhaps find challenging. The majority of them are complex problems that are not amenable to quick or easy answers. You will have to think about them. One level of achievement, perhaps a modest one, is to come up with acceptable answers—acceptable in the judgment of most other able, sane, and conscientious people. A level of achievement up from that is to be able to articulate, with reasonable clarity, why you chose one alternative over another. Still a higher level of ethical competence is to be able to identify all relevant ethical considerations inherent in each problem and then systematically to reason your way through the sometimes baffling maze of real-life possibilities. Perhaps a level higher yet—and one that we do not aspire to here—is to be able to justify your decision making in a manner that would please a professional philosopher, at least to the extent that you would be able to account for your decisions by recourse to one of the well-established ethical approaches that we touch on, briefly, at the conclusion of Chapter 6.

M. Scott Peck's much-celebrated *Road Less Traveled* correctly informs us that life is difficult. It is the moral ambiguity woven into the fabric of existence that largely makes it so.

PART I

A No-Nonsense Primer on Ethics

1

When Titans Stumble

Cases in Corporate Failure

Dry as Dust

To most people, ethics is about the most boring subject on the face of the planet until, because of misconduct, they find themselves in a serious jam, at which point it becomes an exceedingly hot topic and a matter of intense interest—to them and everyone else. Accused of wrongdoing, they wonder, often with considerable amazement and sincere bewilderment, where things went so awry. How in the world, they ask themselves and possibly their attorneys, did they end up in such a mess? Why are *they*—fine, upstanding citizens who intended only to do what was right—now suspected of being foul-hearted villains who, all along, plotted and schemed to do evil? Formerly respected, perhaps revered, how is it that they are now so despised and vilified? Is humanity all that fickle, that predatory and prone to transform itself viciously, individual by individual, from loyal defender to rabid prosecutor? With heads buzzing in agonized confusion, they ruminate and ponder the question: What happened?

There is an old joke according to which one employee asks another, "Do you know why they don't replace us with robots?"

"Why?" asks the second employee.

"Because they couldn't stand the pain!"

When people get into serious legal or ethical trouble, sometimes they can hardly stand the pain. What makes things worse is that the pickle in which they find themselves has usually come on them so unexpectedly.

Everyone is a better-than-average driver. Ask the people around you if you doubt this. Yet half of us, by definition, have to be worse-than-average drivers. So well-developed is our ability to comfort ourselves with flattering self-evaluations that very few of us would classify ourselves in the bottom half of the curve. If we get into a major accident that is our fault, we may soberly rethink our self-assessments, at least for a while. But it usually doesn't take long to rehabilitate our former perceptions of ourselves as expert motor-vehicle operators.

This is pretty much also the reality when it comes to ethics. Many people deem themselves experts, with no need of additional education in what used to be called "moral philosophy," until they do something foolish. And invari-ably, the painful circumstances in which these people find themselves could have been avoided, if only they had known how to navigate the turbulent waters of ethical complexity.

A major purpose of this book is to serve as a practical navigation guide, so that when you face tough ethical questions you will be able to address them with at least some sophistication. Because such questions pop up more often than most people think, it is important to be able to spot moral-ethical con-flicts quickly, so that they don't worm their way into your life without your awareness. It is also important to know how to begin figuring out what to do when these conflicts are complex.

The sorts of ethical problems that prove most troublesome are *not* the rel-atively simple ones covered in formal codes of conduct. It is necessary to know what such codes contain, of course, if for no other reason than to make sure that you steer clear of egregious ethical violations. But knowing the contents of the codes that directly apply to you—those published perhaps by a com-pany for which you work, an association to which you belong, or a profession of which you are a member—is only a starting point. The real art to making wise decisions in the midst of significant personal conflict is to be able to think about ethical issues in an informed manner—in other words, to reason cogently about such conflicts—which in turn means knowing what the deeper issues are and how others before you have thought about them. Often there will be no one clear answer, nothing on the order of a single moral command to tell you what to do.

Insomnia-producing ethical dilemmas do *not* usually embody the kinds of straightforward conflicts or temptations that an intelligent twelve-year-old would recognize and astutely resolve if asked, "What's the right thing to do?" The really thorny ethical challenges are typically subtle, often involve the wel-fare of more than one person or group, characteristically require the rapid and intuitive calculation of probable consequences, and always occur in real time. Their resolution will not wait for you to take a philosophy course at the local junior college, in hopes of quickly picking up some additional wisdom.

If you have had no experience thinking through such challenges, you will be caught flat-footed, and as any veteran boxer will tell you, this is likely to put you squarely on your backside, with your head spinning and your eyes seeing stars. The pages that follow will, I hope, give you plenty of relevant experience. This does not mean that they will necessarily tell you what to do or not to do the next time you confront a difficult ethical choice. It does mean that, if and when this happens, you will know what to watch out for and what important ethical principles to keep in mind as you decide on a course of action.

Public Trust and Human Frailty

Before discussing the tumble from their pedestals of several giants, I again emphasize that everything in this book is based on reports commonly available in the various news media. As of this writing, there have been no criminal convictions in a court of law relating to the companies or persons discussed below, with the exception of one for obstruction of justice.

Global Crossing

As soon as the news broke about Global Crossing's financial troubles, the government of the United States aggressively began to investigate the virtual ruin of this once-touted-by-analysts telecommunications company. No one, certainly none of the individual or institutional investors who lost their shirts when Global Crossing's stock price came tumbling down, expected this. Where were the controls, the checks and balances, and the monitoring mechanisms that are supposed to be in place in every publicly traded company? Where was the protection for shareholders, not to mention employees, many of whom were soon on the street looking for new jobs? Why were there no public disclosures, no significant hints, even, of the company's precarious financial position?

One could argue that Global Crossing simply overreached itself, expanding too rapidly and thus straining capital requirements, and that it was not able accurately to forecast cash flows. It appears that, at the least, the company overbuilt its fiber-optic networks and was subsequently unable to enlist sufficient traffic over those networks to recover its enormous costs. Many objective observers would say that its executives at a minimum oversold the financial outlook of the enterprise to Wall Street analysts. The question, of course, is whether these executives were acting simply out of misplaced optimism or were attempting to mislead. Formal investigations should eventually reveal whether executives at Global Crossing intentionally avoided mandatory financial disclosures. These investigations should also make clear whether there was insider trading, for example, whether certain executives improperly exercised stock options.

The only reason Global Crossing was not even more in the news was that its troubles were soon largely eclipsed in the media by an even bigger scandal.

Enron

Although for the first sixteen years of my career I was a clinical psychologist and a professor—six years in a liberal arts college and ten in a doctoral psychology training program—I have made my living for almost two decades now as a management consultant to senior executives in major corporations. My client companies have included American Airlines, Bell Atlantic, Hunt-Wesson, Price Waterhouse, Raytheon, RAND, Unocal, several once-independent financial institutions (e.g., Bank of America, First Interstate Bank, Home Savings, and Security Pacific Bank) and, more recently, a few online companies and a couple of elite private colleges. But the bulk of my experience as an organizational psychologist has been in the energy industry, which brings me to what at the time was the largest failure in American corporate history and the one that made the decline of Global Crossing seem lightweight by comparison—although it was anything but lightweight to those who suffered as a result.

Until the late fall of 2001, the Cinderella of gas and electric companies was Enron. Throughout the corridors of rival corporations everywhere, executives were looking keenly, admiringly, and often enviously, at "the house that Ken built." As Enron's chief executive officer (CEO), Kenneth Lay was able to transform this once-modest Houston-based enterprise from a mere "one among many" to *the* darling child of Wall Street. Enron's stock price soared to somewhere in the vicinity of $100 per share, and Lay was close to supplanting General Electric's legendary Jack Welch as the country's most celebrated chief executive. Major business periodicals, including but by no means limited to *Forbes*, *Fortune*, and *Business Week*, couldn't get to press fast enough with fawning articles written by otherwise savvy journalists who were so starstruck by Enron's meteoric rise and entrepreneurial chutzpah that you could almost see them pounding the keys of their prose generators, mouths wide open, lower jaws slung down in utter amazement. Enron was too good to be true. Yet there it was, thriving, in living color—demonstrating to a nation that had enjoyed nearly a decade of unrivaled prosperity that American ingenuity, gutsy risk taking, a survival-of-the-fittest competitive mind-set, and good old-fashioned hard work could be combined, brilliantly, to yield unbeatable success as indexed by enormous profits.

As the year 2000 came to a close and a new year began, Enron's investors continued joyfully to calculate their ROIs (returns on investment). But the house that Ken built was beginning to rattle and shake, and after Enron's stock price peaked during the first few months of 2001, it started relentlessly to decline. Could this be? Enron was filled with, and operated by, high rollers, some of them graduates of the most prestigious educational institutions around, including America's elite business schools. Was all this simply too good to be true?

In the summer of 2001, Ken Lay's heir apparent had resigned, abruptly it seemed, having engaged in little if any visible replacement planning. Jeff Skilling had been a consultant with McKinsey & Company, among the most widely esteemed firms of its kind on earth and, in the wry words of some, the applied arm of the Harvard Business School. Skilling, an intellectually gifted but perhaps flawed leader who nonetheless showed prepossessing presence, was recruited by Lay and ultimately succeeded his mentor as CEO (Lay continued on as chairman of the board).

Suddenly, Skilling was gone; not a good sign to those who can think clearly about implications, but such clarity is often in short supply when investors are afflicted with the euphoria that inevitably comes with major financial run-ups. Like scuba divers who, under the intoxicating effects of too much nitrogen, take off their tanks and spit out their regulators in the belief that they no longer need them to breathe, just about anyone connected with Enron assumed that its ever-accelerating profitability would last, if not forever then certainly well beyond whatever time they would need to cash out.

For months on end, America struggled to come to terms with its biggest corporate failure in its history. Enron filed for bankruptcy in December 2001, in a manner that departed radically from its traditional spotlight-seeking style. As a friend of mine observed, quietly filing for Chapter 11 bankruptcy in New York, rather than in Houston where it was headquartered, gave Enron more the look of a small company fleeing creditors than of the industry-dominant corporation that it had been for years.

An extraordinary amount of congressional time and energy has been devoted to unraveling the mystery of how such a thing could have happened in twenty-first-century America. It's not just that a leading company tumbled from its lofty pedestal as the seventh largest enterprise in the United States. Everyone knows that success entails risk and that businesses occasionally fail. What made this particular failure so hard to stomach was the egregious conduct that seems to have precipitated it. Skilling, against his attorney's advice to "take the Fifth," defiantly insisted that he did nothing wrong; Lay claimed to have known nothing about what was going on right under his nose; and Enron's chief financial officer, Andrew Fastow, seems to have said nothing of substance in answer to the question of how one share of Enron's stock was, subsequent to Enron's collapse, worth less than a dollar.

The merciless crash of most dotcom companies only a year or two earlier had nothing on Enron; wise investors, unconvinced by the underlying business models and associated value propositions (Value = Benefits — Cost) of most dotcoms, had expected their downfall all along. Even the more pervasive and enduring stock market crash of 1929, or for that matter the collapse three centuries earlier of the tulip market in Amsterdam, which left many previously affluent speculators close to destitute, couldn't match the Enron debacle. In 1929 there were few controls on buying shares on credit ("margin"); you could borrow as much as 90 percent of the purchase price from the brokerage house, and why not? Everyone knew that the stock market would continue to rise. A large percentage of middle-class Americans, fancying themselves in possession of the shrewdness of a robber baron, naively "played the market" in the expectation that it would sustain, at most, only minor setbacks ("corrections"). The actual results, of course, were devastating to them, the country, and—some would argue—the global economy.

Going on eighty years later, most Americans assume that well-thought-out rules and regulations make such catastrophes impossible today. And viewing the American economy as a whole, perhaps they are. The effects of Enron's demise were, after all, localized. It wasn't as if America's entire economy came tumbling down. Yet such wide-angle commentary provides little comfort to those whose economic lives were ruined when what had been worth $100,000 plummeted to a value of under $1,000.

Thousands of Enron employees lost most of their pensions and, in many cases, nearly all their net worth—their personal fortunes. I can still vividly picture the faces of former Enron employees on television. Trying to hold back the tears leaking from the corners of his eyes, one man said that it was a terrible thing to be poor, which was the condition in which he and his wife now found themselves. "We used to shop at department stores," he muttered in pain. "Now we go to the thrift shop." Another said, "I expected someday to be able to retire—it's hard to face the fact that, now, I'll have to work for the rest of my life." No high rollers here; just ordinary people, like you and me, who trusted business leaders to do right by them. Money accumulated through hard work over the course of years simply vanished. And predictably, there seem to have been suicides as a result, just as there were when the crash in October 1929 kicked off the Great Depression. It is not easy to see one's hope of retiring go up in smoke. The great American dream of being able someday to enjoy the fruits of one's labors was, for many, blown to smithereens.

An especially bitter pill to swallow for Enron's ex-employees was that top executives appear to have encouraged them to purchase additional shares of company stock while these same executives were quietly selling off their own shares. Ken's house was about to crumble, and it seems that the upper echelons knew it. If, as Daniel Goleman suggested in *Emotional Intelligence* (1995), the earmark of a sociopath is an absence of empathy, you have to wonder about some of Enron's leaders, because empathy was clearly not their strong suit. They appear to have been singularly unconcerned about widows and orphans.

Another bitter pill—and one that could choke the proverbial horse—is that Enron's auditing firm was Arthur Andersen. Prior to the Enron scandal, people generally trusted such entities. If a prestigious accounting firm certified that a corporation's financial position was solid, most investors took this at face value; whether they do anymore remains to be seen. When it surfaced that Arthur Andersen's employees seem to have intentionally destroyed thousands of Enron-related documents, the public was first horrified, then outraged. For a public accounting firm to do such a thing is like a town fire marshal turning out to be an arsonist.

Since these events unfolded, the Securities and Exchange Commission (SEC) has belatedly decreed that an accounting firm may not provide both auditing and consulting services to the same company, which is what Arthur Andersen had been doing with Enron. It takes no theoretical physicist to figure out that an accounting firm that is charging millions of dollars each year for its "consulting" advice may be exceedingly reluctant to antagonize the leaders of that corporate client by questioning the integrity of its financial statements. Turning things around, if you were the CEO of a large corporation that was playing it close to or over the line, perhaps by engaging in questionable accounting practices, might you be tempted to hire and pay handsomely "consultants" from the accounting firm that audits your company? Such consultants might, at the very least, be motivated to "calm down" any auditor who became excessively scrupulous in the performance of his or her duties; they would certainly have the power to do so if, for example, such an auditor had not yet come to understand the importance of "good client relations." That it took the Enron debacle to motivate the SEC, finally, to put an end to such conflicts is, in my judgment, nothing short of amazing.

What is most poignant about what happened with Enron is how flagrantly executives from both Enron and Arthur Andersen failed to carry out their ethical duties. For different but related reasons, both Enron's executives and Arthur Andersen's accountants bore considerable "fiduciary" responsibility: they held special positions of trust and were relied on by their various publics to prove worthy of this trust.

Holders of Enron stock expected, at a minimum, to be told the truth about the financial condition of the company. It certainly seems misleading, for example, to encourage employees to buy more shares when you have information to suggest that the value of these shares is likely to decline. It is no secret that the annual reports of most, if not all, publicly traded corporations cast these companies in a favorable light. The glass is routinely half full, never half empty, and profitability over the long haul is surely going to increase. While one might question whether such puffery is honorable, just about everyone knows that it goes on and pretty much expects it. What we do *not* expect is fraud. We do not expect to be intentionally misled into doing things that will hurt us. The last thing we expect an executive in our own company to do is to sacrifice us on the altar of buoying up the price per share of a failing enterprise built on one shaky deal after another. Did Enron, as an entity, or its executives engage in fraud? Time and the courts will tell.

The fiduciary responsibility carried by a public accounting firm is at least as great as that carried by a traditional business, and some would say greater. A company's financial statements, including but not limited to its annual report, are supposed to be accurate and to disclose anything that is material to its present or anticipated financial outcomes. It is the auditing firm's job to make sure this is the case, and many different groups depend on it to do this job honestly, competently, and conscientiously: individual investors, investment fund managers, securities analysts, employees of the company, directors and officers who may be held personally liable for mismanagement, firms that underwrite insurance against potential loss, financial institutions that either rate the company's creditworthiness or lend it money, and, as representative of us all, various levels of government.

So what went wrong? How did a company that in early 2001 was still the darling child of Wall Street, led by one of the most admired executives in America, end up in shambles, with never a hint given of its impending collapse? And how did a colossal and eminently respected accounting firm end up serving as what seems to have been an accomplice to such a gross betrayal of the public trust?

WorldCom and a Host of Other Companies

Since the troubles within Enron came to light, questions have been raised or allegations made about many other companies. WorldCom's financial losses more than doubled those of Enron's, and some would argue that its conduct was even more disturbing, since it seems to have involved misrepresenting nearly $4 billion of expenses as "investments." This is similar to telling your investors that your company spent $1 million buying a building (which still has a value and can be depreciated over time) when, in reality, you spent it to pay your rent—except that the $3.8 billion that WorldCom allegedly "invested" is 3,800 times $1 million! That would give even the richest sheik some indigestion.

Yet what transpired at WorldCom, however astonishing and possibly unlawful, is relatively straightforward when compared to what occurred at Enron. There seems to have been little ethical subtlety to it. The Enron case, and everything that surrounded it, is far richer in content and therefore far more interesting, and so we will use it as the basis for much of the discussion that follows. What happened at Enron—perhaps more than any other set of events—prompted considerable outrage on the part of the general public about the conduct of American business and a corresponding concern for ethical reform that is likely to be salient for many years to come.

Identifying the Issues

Reading about the ruination of "fortunes" may cause you to picture wealthy executives who own multimillion-dollar houses in gated communities, ride in well-waxed black limousines, and hire chauffeurs who double as muscle-bound bodyguards. Who cares, you might be asking yourself, if such fat cats take a hit to their portfolios, or even receive a good financial trouncing? They can always find other lucrative jobs and in a few years make back whatever they lost. So what if they can't shop at Neiman-Marcus or Nordstrom for a while? Or if they can't buy their kids new red BMWs when they turn sixteen? Life is tough all over! It was their choice, after all, to sit at a high-stakes poker table. Let *them* eat cake for once. No sniveling allowed.

Those whose fortunes were ruined were, in the vast majority of cases, not the nobles but the serfs, the "working stiffs" as they (we) are occasionally called, those of us who usually pay our monthly bills with the money we earned in the preceding month—not cash "thrown off" by accumulated capital. To the extent that we have any capital socked away, it is either in the form of retirement funds or home equity, and the latter mostly doesn't count because, after all, we have to live somewhere. And, likely as not, if we work for a publicly traded company, in contrast to a small business, not-for-profit entity, or the government, our retirement money is substantially if not totally invested in the company—well, perhaps not, post-Enron.

Of itself, the losses investors have suffered, however great and personally traumatic, do not suggest, much less prove, any moral wrongdoing, a point made earlier. All investments, by definition, involve risk. Companies rise and fall every day, and so does the net worth of individual owners: shareholders, in the case of publicly traded companies. Yet certain aspects of Enron's failure are especially troubling. Although I have mentioned some of them already, I want to summarize these aspects more systematically and also point to a number of wider implications. So many interesting and complex issues have emerged from the Enron case that it provides us with perhaps the richest case study in corporate ethics to have come along in decades.

1. Senior leaders at Enron appear to have actively encouraged employees to purchase shares, even after these leaders appear to have known that a decline in price, if not an outright collapse of the company, was imminent. One motive for such advocacy, to the extent that it took place, may have been to ward off any downward spiral in price per share that might occur as soon as word began to leak out about the company's true financial condition.

2. Even more reprehensible was the fact that, apparently, some of the people who were puffing the value of Enron's stock to trusting employees were themselves selling off their own holdings in the company. If Enron's price per share were all that certain to increase, why were they selling their shares in such large quantities while holding rah-rah rallies for employees, designed in part to advertise the excellence of Enron as an investment?

3. There seems to be little doubt, at this point, that Enron had entered into a number of unfavorable agreements (contracts) that at the least were unprofitable. In the aggregate, these contracts were costing the company substantial sums of money. Instead of owning up to the losses, which is what ethical and perhaps legal standards of conduct would demand, it appears that one or more senior executives did everything they could to avoid taking "write-downs" (declared losses). Technically, these losses were recorded in off-balance-sheet partnerships—partnerships backed by Enron stock. Many congressional hearings have been conducted, with no small amount of self-righteous grandstanding by some of our more publicity-hungry politicians, and it will eventually be up to the courts to determine how much culpability, if any, resides in the souls of Ken Lay, Jeff Skilling, and Andrew Fastow. We don't, however, need a court to make clear the obvious: Enron was anything but forthcoming in all of this.

4. Part of what appears to have been the deliberate misrepresentation of Enron's financial health was a now-infamous conference call with Wall Street analysts, the people charged, in part, with the responsibility for analyzing publicly traded companies for investment-worthiness. Fully cognizant of its ailing and potentially fatal condition, its senior spokespersons seem to have reassured the analysts in October 2001 of Enron's robustness. They also allegedly proclaimed their full support of Chief Financial Officer Andrew Fastow, who was fired, according to reports, the very next day. Their behavior was perhaps tantamount to

discovering that you have an especially virulent form of cancer and concealing this fact from a physician in order to qualify for a huge life insurance policy. (Defrauding an insurance company, by the way, is a significant crime.) While it could be argued that these analysts should have been astute enough to determine the true condition of Enron, perhaps by digging more diligently, the moral burden, and perhaps the legal one as well, clearly resided with Enron, not Wall Street.

5. The near demise of Enron has turned the searchlight of ethical scrutiny more pointedly than ever on two groups of professionals, one of whom are the very same sorts of financial analysts who were so quick to cry "foul" when they learned the deeper truths about Enron. Although the economy of the United States enjoyed unprecedented growth throughout most of the 1990s, as reflected for example in the exponential growth of the various stock markets, it has been more or less stalled for some time now, and no one of any widely acclaimed expertise is predicting a fast turnaround. Yet today, as has been true for a long time, most securities analysts have attached either a "hold" or a "buy" recommendation on virtually all securities traded on the New York Stock Exchange (NYSE). Only about 1 percent—again, perhaps slightly higher post-Enron—of the companies followed by these analysts have managed to earn a "sell" rating, which most knowledgeable people suggest smells fishier than a tuna factory. It is also widely known among corporate financial executives that brokerage houses that "have a market in" (underwrite and promote) a particular security routinely hawk its value as an investment through in-house specialists who, on occasion, go public about the dilemma they encounter under pressure to write what they should to sustain their upward mobility, on the one hand, or what they should to honor the dictates of their consciences. One such analyst recently admitted that he energetically advised the firm's clients to purchase a stock that, in a private memorandum, he described to a colleague as a financial "joke." The absence of laughter on the faces of those who followed his fraudulent recommendation helped trigger an investigation by the SEC into the conduct of financial analysts, and the brokerage houses for which they typically work, the likes of which our country has not witnessed since the early 1930s.

6. The other group of professionals currently on the hot seat are accountants, more specifically, accounting firms that offer both auditing and consulting services, often to the same corporate client. What Enron was doing appears to have been, in the opinion of its worst critics, a kind of Ponzi (pyramid) scheme, according to which money from new investors (e.g., partners) was more or less used to pay monies owed to previous

investors. Such arrangements work as long as you continue to recruit additional investors, usually at an ever-increasing rate, so that you can keep the whole thing going. Arthur Andersen was the accounting firm hired by Enron to audit, and by implication to certify, the trustworthiness of its financial statements (e.g., its annual report to shareholders). As such, Arthur Andersen should have known that something was seriously amiss. Judging from the fact that the Andersen partner who seems to have been in charge of the Enron golden goose agreed to become a witness for the prosecution in return for certain immunities from prosecution and, in the process, admitted to having intentionally destroyed documents, it appears that the accounting firm did know about Enron's arrangements. The question of the hour, if not the decade, has been why the very firm charged by the public with the fiduciary duty to disclose such facts apparently did the opposite. Many suggest that this was because Arthur Andersen was also charging Enron substantial fees for "management consulting" services. Had the auditors disclosed what at least some of them knew, it is likely that Arthur Andersen would have suffered a double whammy. I suspect that it would have been fired as a consultant (in the language of the consulting business, their contract would not have been renewed or continued), and all future audits would probably have been awarded to a competing firm, perhaps a "smarter" enterprise that was more hungry for the Enron account and therefore less inclined to prove scrupulous and troublesome. Having the same accounting firm supply both auditing and consulting services is a bit like having the judge in a legal proceeding in the employ of the attorney for the defense. Such a dual arrangement, as it turns out, is not all that uncommon, and a case can be made that it is functional because the firm already knows the client company and how it operates. It also knows the challenges, often complex, that the company faces, so it doesn't have to claw its way up a steep learning curve—at the client's expense. Yet, as we shall see, such monetary savings are achieved at the cost of compromising a fundamental principle that lies at the heart of virtually all codes of ethics.

7. This brings us, finally, to another form of questionable professional conduct, although I am not at all sure it will ever be remedied; I am not even sure it should be. This has to do with the implicit versus the explicit services provided by certain management-consulting firms. Exceedingly bright people, usually MBAs but sometimes CPAs or attorneys, educated at top universities populate these firms. So far, so good. But there is a subtle rub. Although people who serve on the boards of large corporations are often, but by no means always, wealthy, they are not eager

to part unnecessarily with their own money. They are least eager to part with it as a result of predatory class-action lawsuits organized by professional "green-mailers," who make mega-incomes from the fees "earned" from huge settlements sometimes offered by corporations to ensure that such suits never make it to court. Virtually all corporations of any substance carry "D&O" liability insurance, designed to cover Directors (members of the board) and Officers (senior executives) in the event of alleged or actual negligence. If a court of law determines that a member of a company's board was negligent (think "deep pocket" here) because of something he or she did or failed to do, the respondent (director) will be required to pay damages, not to speak of having to hire a stable of top-notch lawyers to fight the suit in the first place. All insurance policies stipulate coverage limits, which means that directors are always at personal financial risk, particularly since certain groups of people seem increasingly prone to join such suits (e.g., shareholders alleging that the value of their holdings has been diminished as a direct result of managerial incompetence). The way it really works, according to the agreement customarily entered into when a person agrees to serve as an officer or director, is that, once the limits of D&O insurance are exceeded, the corporation's assets are used to pay the overage. This, however, does not entirely assuage the anxiety, even the panic, that officers and directors experience when they detect the ominous footsteps of a green-mailer. If, for example, the limit on the D&O liability policy is $150 million, the corporation's assets come to $125 million, and the courts award $450 million, then even after liquidation of the company, someone has to come up with the missing $175 million—and guess who those "someones" are. If gross negligence is alleged and sustained by the court, additional "punitive" damages may be awarded, since the courts view such negligence as so egregious that it is equivalent to malice. An example would be a surgeon operating on a patient while still intoxicated from an alcoholic binge he or she went on the night before. The consulting firms to which I have alluded reduce the vulnerability of directors and officers by putting their imprimatur on important decisions, typically by doing an expensive (seven-figure fees are common) and well-executed study that, more often than not, leads to the conclusion that the company should proceed in the direction that its top leaders envisioned in the first place. It is something of a sardonic joke that the best consultants are the best listeners, that is, that they "recognize right answer when told" and, in the conduct of whatever analysis they undertake, are able to pull together enough "data" supplied by mid-level employees to justify that answer with great credibility. On its face this might seem scandalous, except for the fact that most of the time senior executives of mainline companies, and many of *their* subordinates, do know what to do; so much so that these subordinates, and often their subordinates, commonly complain that they freely shared information and perspectives with consultants, only to see their creative work repackaged as "the result of six months of careful study"—without, in their view, sufficient credit being given to the in-house experts who, out of loyalty to the enterprise, opened the doors of their intellectual cupboards. Such reactions, while understandable, do not reckon with the fact that sometimes consulting companies are in the business of selling supplemental liability protection every bit as much as pristine objective analysis. In terms of liability avoidance, their imprimaturs are often worth far more than the considerable fees they charge for their vetting services. This is not to say that the consultants working for such firms are lazy. Far from it; they may work eighty-hour weeks in a valiant quest for intellectual excellence and are often committed to due diligence. It is to say, however, that sometimes there is a second transaction going on, albeit on the margins of consciousness, and that this transaction has little to do with the unfettered search for truth.

In the next chapter, we examine the relationship between law and ethics. Are illegal acts by definition unethical? Are all unethical acts illegal? Is it possible to stay within the bounds of the law and still be a scoundrel?

2

Law, Ethics, and Society

The Relationship between Law and Ethics

Most people would agree that committing a crime is generally a bad thing to do and hence that whatever is illegal is, by definition, also unethical. There are instances in which laws are neither ethical nor unethical (e.g., declaring a building a historic landmark, rules for certain legal proceedings) and others in which breaking the law would be morally superior to not breaking it (e.g., driving the wrong way on a one-street to avoid hitting a pedestrian, breaking the speed laws to get someone to the hospital quickly), but you'd have to be a pretty hard-nosed anarchist or a nihilist to argue that such instances were the rule rather than the exception.

Laws generally embody what society regards as right conduct. Violating most laws, from perpetrating violent crimes to breaking local ordinances against turning your radio up too loud, is generally considered "bad." We may all commit minor "crimes" once in a while, such as coasting through a stop sign or driving a bit above the speed limit, but few of us would seriously attempt to argue that this sort of behavior is good. Most of our laws are intended to bring about the greatest amount of good for people overall. They are thus what philosophers would call "utilitarian" in their intent.

Many acts that seem patently unethical to most sane adults are not, however, illegal. They may embarrass you, but they will not land you in jail. Edging your car forward to prevent another vehicle from entering your lane of traffic is not illegal, and we have probably all done this from time to time, but we would not hold this up as a model of altruism. Nor would we especially enjoy seeing ourselves on television while engaging in such a selfishly competitive action.

21

Sometimes the line between "unethical" and "illegal" is a blurry one. For example, the law allows a certain amount of what is usually called "puffery" or exaggeration ("hype") by those trying to sell products. It is almost always perfectly legal to claim that whatever it is you are selling is "wonderful," that it will bring complete customer "satisfaction," even that it is the "best on the market"—even if it is the worst. It is not legal, however, to claim that the black box you are selling for $19.95 will turn pennies into quarters and thus make the purchaser wealthy. Such a claim would be fraudulent and quickly land you in jail. The question is where to draw the line between puffery and intentional deceit.

It is worth noting in passing that the technical difference between fraud and misrepresentation is that fraud involves intent. It is possible to misrepresent something to, and therefore to mislead, another person without realizing that you're doing it. If, for example, your sales manager has told you that the laundry detergent you have just begun to sell will remove all traces of red wine that has been spilled on white dress shirts when, in fact, the substance is totally useless for this purpose, and you innocently relate this information to a customer who buys a case of it from you, you have committed no crime— although your manager may have. You will probably feel terrible when you learn about having unwittingly misled the customer but, regardless of how angry he becomes, you have done nothing illegal or unethical. To the contrary, you acted in good faith.

The difference between breaking a law and doing something that is legal but unethical is a bit like the difference between lies of commission and omission. Most of us would readily agree that telling lies is, in general, wrong. Yet many people who would find themselves outraged if someone close to them told a flat-out falsehood, and who would rarely, if ever, tell a lie themselves, have no hesitancy whatever in withholding information, sometimes to the obvious detriment of others. Telling a lie is, to them, breaking a moral law, while not telling the complete truth is not. Although it is easy to come up with situations in which withholding information is probably superior to volunteering it, such withholding more often than not leads other people to draw false conclusions and to make decisions that may not be in their interests. When corporate officers omit relevant facts for the purpose of deceiving investors, they are acting both unethically and illegally. The same is true for testimony in a court of law, where one swears to tell the "whole" truth.

Suppose, for example, that you own a home on a lake, in a highly desirable area—the "high rent" district—and you decide to sell your house. A day after listing the property with a real estate broker, you discover that the person who owns the house in front of yours, the one between your home and the lake, is thinking about adding a second story. If the neighbor does this, it will totally obscure the view of the water from your property. The question becomes whether you will disclose this information to potential buyers. If you do, the sale price will surely be lower. You could withhold the information, consoling yourself with the notion of *caveat emptor* ("buyer beware"), especially since you are under no legal obligation to discuss what may only amount to your neighbor's "possibility thinking." Yet, if you withhold it, are you not lying by omission and, if so, are you not every bit as culpable as the pathological fabricator or confidence man who would, if he could, part you from the contents of your wallet?

The analogy between overt and covert lies, on the one hand, and law and ethics, on the other, breaks down if pushed too far, however, because even the law recognizes that the refusal to provide information under certain circumstances is unacceptable and against public policy, that is, not good for society at large. This is why, except in unusual circumstances such as when asked to testify against a spouse or taking the relatively drastic step of "pleading the Fifth," people do not have the option of refusing to testify. It is also why "disclosure laws" apply to just about all real estate transactions. The boundaries between the illegal and the unethical are, in certain arenas, fuzzy indeed. Our analogy also breaks down because there are instances in which lies of omission are every bit as grievous, and sometimes more so, than lies of commission.

We do not "elect" to follow society's laws, rules, and regulations (e.g., the Internal Revenue Service tax code). They are more or less imposed on us, in pursuit of the general good. Subscribing to formal codes of ethics, adhering to a loosely connected set of ethical principles (e.g., what you learned at the feet of your parents), or rigorously attempting to make all moral decisions in accordance with a specific philosophical or religious worldview are all, more or less, voluntary postures. Failure to meet specific ethical standards—standards of goodness—may cause you to lose your job or to be expelled from a professional society. It may even cause you to forfeit a hard-won license to practice your chosen profession, if licensure in your state has been linked to *not* getting thrown out of a national association (e.g., a psychologist who lost membership in the American Psychological Association as a direct result of ethical misconduct would be hard pressed to retain the right to practice in California). Ethical violations of themselves, however, will not earn you a berth in jail or prison unless these violations were illegal, which usually they are not. They may cause others to raise their eyebrows in disdain or disgust and, if your technically legal but morally deplorable conduct is sufficiently offensive, you may become an outcast. But you will not become a convict.

Governments, Laws, and Ethical Duties

The notion that laws and the governmental structures that uphold them are both necessary and desirable goes back a long way. Two thousand years ago, the New Testament writer Paul suggested that the existence of governments, and by implication social organizations that protect people in general from predatory behavior by individuals or groups, are integral to human existence and should be honored (see Rom. 13:1–7). Hundreds of years before that, Greek philosophers had, for the most part, reached the conclusion that good government is moral, and they devoted considerable time and energy to figuring out and articulating the characteristics of such government (e.g., Plato's *Republic*, which extols the virtues of philosopher-kings). And from the dawn of civilization, which one may somewhat arbitrarily define as the advent of agriculture and nonnomadic villages (roughly twelve thousand years ago), *homo sapiens* voted with their behavior for the existence of rules by which most, ideally all, members of a given society would live and coexist. That there have been an abundance of bad governments and countless individuals who, in the name of benevolence, have used their socially sanctioned authority to do all manner of evil cannot be denied. But, just as the occasional rotting of food by bacteria does not alter the reality that food is in general good, indeed essential to human survival, so rancid governments, unjust laws, and malevolent rulers do not impugn the value, in fact the necessity, of governments, laws, or officials.

People who evade their responsibility as citizens to support the social order reflected in just governments and their laws are cheating the other members of their societies. They want the benefits without the costs and the protections without the obligations. Whether they wear hand-tailored suits made of Italian silk or blue jeans with holes in them, whether they prey on others through clever financial schemes or the more primitive use of switchblades, they are mavericks, rebels, and to a greater or lesser extent enemies of the body politic. If truth be told, we are all from time to time, at least to a tiny extent, mavericks, rebels, and enemies of the populace at large. It can be easy, however, to become these things more rapidly and extensively than we ever thought possible. One purpose of this book is to make such ugly transformations less likely.

When people flout the norms by which our society has bound itself through laws or, more loosely, through certain ethical standards, they are usually turning their backs on their duties to humankind.

Ethical Codes

As human beings, we have what may be an innate appreciation for goodness. Just as we seem inherently to love physical beauty, however we may define it, we seem also—most of us, anyway—to love moral beauty (however we define that). Few people would debate that we should strive to do good. The hard part sometimes comes in deciding exactly what goodness ("moral beauty") would look like in a concrete, real-life situation, especially if the realities of circumstance compel one to choose among the lesser of several evils or the greater of several goods. Ethical codes and philosophical systems of ethics are intended to help, and often they do.

Ethics, like laws, exist to bring out the best in us and, in the process, to assist society and perhaps even to advance civilization. They tell us what others at large perceive to be our moral obligations. But while laws usually make abundantly clear what we *cannot* do (at least not without consequences if detected), and codes of ethics, because they do the same sort of thing, are *relatively* easy to apply, systems of ethics are often difficult to translate from theory into practice. This is because ethical philosophies—what I mean by "systems"—are intended to provide us with a more sophisticated form of assistance. They offer a coherent approach to values, a way to tell whether "this" is more important than "that" when the hurricanes of moral confusion quickly come upon us. Some of the greatest minds in history have attempted to provide us with help, lest we founder on the rocks of despair when the storms of complex ethical choice rage all around, not least in our own hearts and minds. Driven to our knees, sometimes half-broken by the realization that we simply do not know, indeed cannot know for sure, we cry to the heavens, "What shall I do now?"

The sort of thing that a code of ethics makes clear is demonstrated with an illustration from the medical profession. According to an interpretive addendum to the American Medical Association's (AMA's) code of ethics, physicians are not supposed to accept gifts of significant material value from pharmaceutical companies or their representatives. Even if every medical doctor in the country were in the habit of breaking this rule, there would still be little confusion as to its intent or meaning: the AMA doesn't want physicians to feel inappropriately obligated to prescribe one drug over another or to prescribe a drug when no medication is warranted; the doctor's *only* consideration in making a medication decision should be what's best for the patient. As suggested above, a bright adolescent could easily read, interpret, and apply the "rule."

Once you move much beyond formal codes and their associated commentaries, you land squarely in the philosopher's, and perhaps the theologian's, backyard. Ethical codes and commentaries function, as suggested earlier, as (sometimes softly enforced) laws for those bound to observe them. But their scope is always limited to the basics, and real-life ethical decisions can prove heart-wrenching because of their mind-boggling ambiguity.

3

Threats, Risks, and Options

Pressures and Vulnerabilities

Are foul deeds committed by "bad" people, whereas good people, like us, would never—could never—think of doing such things? Or is the reality more complex?

Are we really all that different from most of Enron's executives or from Arthur Andersen's accountants and consultants? If we assume that we are somehow morally superior to the rest of humanity, we are lulling ourselves into moral slumber and, in the process, leaving ourselves unnecessarily vulnerable. However much we may like to delude ourselves with self-righteous assertions, we all do bad things. Maybe what we do is nowhere near as bad as what Enron's executives seem to have done. On the other hand, under the pressures that they felt, we might have been swept along by roaring crosscurrents and ferocious tides, and done worse! You never truly know what you will do under pressure—pressure that brings with it real and substantial consequences—until you're actually in the situation. This, by the way, is the key message resounding through a great deal of the world's finest literature, from Shakespeare's *Hamlet* to Joseph Conrad's *Lord Jim*.

As the ex-CEO of a large energy company said to me not long ago, "I learned never to underestimate the power of greed or ambition." True, we might have been more conciliatory when questioned by members of Congress than Jeff Skilling has been. And our alarm bells might have gone off earlier when faced by tough choices that threatened to compromise us. But, as people, are we not all cut from the same human cloth? Do we not all share essentially the same genetic material? Are we not, all of us, at least a little greedy and a bit overambitious?

26

The higher you climb up the ladder of any organization, and perhaps the greater your compensation, the more you will find yourself subject to awkward and uncomfortable pressures. This, I strongly believe, is the nature of things. If you have a low-level job, no one is going to ask you to do much beyond your assigned duties. You may be subject to other kinds of unpleasantries, such as unwanted sexual advances or getting assigned to a committee whose chairperson you'd prefer to avoid, but it is unlikely that anyone will stop by to see what you're doing, personally, to "grow the organization" or augment its revenues.

But this is not the case for people with major management responsibilities, even those who work for not-for-profit corporations; even in nonprofit organizations, leaders are often expected to increase membership, solicit donations, solidify the entity's position of power vis-à-vis its rivals, appear fiscally sound to potential contributors and regulatory agencies, and justify its decisions to a sometimes suspicious public that seems to spawn watchdog groups faster than teenage rock bands.

Executives in traditional corporations or professional service firms, such as Enron and Arthur Andersen, are customarily expected to increase the company's or firm's after-tax profits and to ensure that its price per share or fee-for-service billing level increases. At a minimum, the stock price of a publicly traded company must not be allowed to decline very far, because for every dollar it does, the "capitalization" of the corporation declines by millions of dollars. Nor, in a service firm, must its annual revenues decline. Shareholders, whether individuals or institutions, tend to take a dim view of declining stock prices, and some of them can be more troublesome than an enraged hornet, especially at shareholder meetings or, worse, in courts of law. And managing partners may well put you on the street, even after decades of loyal service, if you fail to produce. Imagine for a moment that the stock price will go up or down by $23 a share, depending on how you resolve a fuzzy ethical dilemma. Not a clear case of right or wrong, you reason, but the kind of decision that could keep you up all night over what to do and the likely consequences to you if you do this versus that. Imagine also that you are in charge of a huge account; keeping it rests largely on making the client happy; there are some marginally questionable things going on—and if you bring them to light, in contrast to ignoring them, you will lose your job, default on your mortgage, be viewed as having been fired by everyone you know, and perhaps be branded via your industry's grapevine as a marginal performer who "doesn't have what it takes."

Even Navy SEALS Disobey Orders

Many people believe that men and women in the military cannot disobey direct orders and that, if they do, severe consequences will follow. And sometimes they do. Yet, as films such as *Crimson Tide* suggest, even persons in the military have to make moral judgments that might, on occasion, lead them *not* to do what they are told. In point of fact, military personnel, according to the Uniform Code of Military Justice (UCMJ), may not carry out an unlawful order.

I once asked a naval officer, a SEAL, if he had ever flatly refused to do something he was ordered to do. To my surprise, he said that a more senior officer from another branch of the service once wanted him to conduct a mission that he believed would unnecessarily jeopardize the lives of his men. Although he provided no details—nor did I ask for any—he told me that he had simply refused. "I may have paid a political price that will come back to haunt me someday," he added, "but I did what I thought was right." In this instance, the order was not illegal, just imprudent.

There are times when you have to vote your conscience rather than your career. For him, this was one of those times.

When Not to Be a Team Player

Among the greatest pressures on people who work for organizations, especially large ones, is to be team players in contrast to individualists. Just yesterday I received a résumé from a woman who is currently looking for an executive position and wants my assistance. On it in bold type were the words "good team player."

Of itself, nothing is wrong with wanting employees at all levels of an organization to work well together and to view themselves as members of a team. Even if they are in jobs for "individual contributors," such as certain technical analyst positions, it is usually desirable for them to regard their contributions as part of a larger effort and to be willing, as circumstances may demand, to subordinate their individualistic goals to those of the overall organization.

The problem is that this emphasis on teamwork can be used in insidious ways. In some social and professional circles, it is almost the kiss of death to call someone's behavior "inappropriate." This seems like a relatively harmless thing to say, and yet, it can prove lethal to another person's social or professional standing. In a lot of companies, it is just as pernicious, and perhaps more, to say that so-and-so is "not a team player." As a result, a good number of employees run with a certain measure of fear that this will be said of them—which makes them exceedingly vulnerable to manipulation.

If you sense that you are being maneuvered into doing something that you do not want to do (perhaps something that you shouldn't do) by the subtle threat that someone will say that you are not a good team player, the alarm bells in your head should go off immediately. And if the person attempting to manipulate you in this manner is your supervisor, (1) you have a serious problem to deal with, and (2) you should probably discuss the matter, quickly, with a wise person whom you trust.

Saying No and Meaning It

It sometimes happens that another person will try to get you to do something that you believe is ethically questionable, and this person is likely to be someone in a position of power. The stakes could be high. Yet, without thinking about it for more than a nanosecond, you may be able to refuse. Let me add that I recommend you do this tactfully. Avoid such utterances as "Are you kidding? You're asking me to do that? You must be out of your mind." You might want to say something along the lines of "I don't feel comfortable doing that." The wonderful thing about saying that you do not feel comfortable is that you can come back to it, again and again, without explanation. If, for example, the other person asks, "Why not? Why does that make you uncomfortable?" you always have the option of saying, "I'm not sure, but I'm just not comfortable."

Instinctively, you may know that if you go along with the request, even a little, it will open the door to further compromise. It is not just that what you are being asked to do is wrong. In each particular case, maybe it is and maybe it isn't—although in your "gut" you may feel sure that it is. On a practical level, your thinking may proceed along these lines: "This doesn't feel right. In fact, it feels downright wrong. When in doubt . . . don't! If I do it anyway and later decide that it *was* wrong, I'll be in a pickle. I can always change my 'no' to 'yes' later if I want, but it will be a lot harder to retract a commitment I've made." There will probably be few instances when you later decide to do something that you initially felt to be unethical.

The time to put an end to going down the wrong path is before you set foot on it. It is a little like the conventional wisdom about how to handle a potential blackmailer: not one thin dime! Take whatever lumps you are going to take right away because, if you start paying, you'll never be able to stop.

Peremptory Decisions

The principal meaning of the word *peremptory* is stopping or preventing debate. Using his or her peremptory challenges, an attorney can often dismiss a certain number of jurors, for example, without producing a reason—there is no discussion whatever about cause or the lack of it. To a certain extent you can do the same sort of thing in everyday life, and this can be tremendously helpful. An executive I know, Darcel L. Hulse, put it this way: "You make the decision one time in advance." Hulse also said, "Winning is not about toys but about character."

One peremptory decision you might want to make is this: "I will do nothing criminal in the course of my work, no matter how dire the circumstances." You may think this is a no-brainer, but I can assure you that you are probably a lot clearer about this issue now, sitting in an easy chair, than you would be if your boss told you that the company was counting on you, you were its only hope, and all that would be required to save it was for you to sign certain documents—no one would ever know. This was precisely one of the dilemmas portrayed in the recent film *Changing Lanes*. The beauty of peremptory decision making is that you can decide when your head is clear and you're under no pressure.

Here is another peremptory decision you might want to make: "I will resign my job before sacrificing my integrity." Exactly what you mean by "integrity" may not be all that easy to define, certainly not to the satisfaction of a philosopher. And to the extent that you are unclear about its meaning, you may be inclined to vacillate when put to the test. It is therefore worthwhile to give as much cool-headed thought as you can to what you mean by integrity, so that you have at least a reasonably clear idea of what it means to maintain it; there will always be room for clarification. Still, there may be things to decide, now, that you will never do—regardless of who asks or what it costs you.

Time to Stay and Time to Go

Organizations change over time, so that your company or institution may hardly resemble the one you joined ten years ago. The difficulty is that such changes typically occur gradually. They can, of course, happen quickly, perhaps on the heels of a lopsided merger or straight-out acquisition. But most of the time organizations change as children grow: little by little.

As a couple of Stanford Business School professors[1] have pointed out, the values of an organization are not so much created as discovered. It is naive to think that you can instill values in an organization simply by writing up a spiffy document, posting it on the wall, and getting people to carry laminated cards around in their wallets. There is merit to these sorts of activities, as long as you recognize that whatever you publish and promote along these lines is, at best, a set of aspirations.

When you discover that the values of the organization you work for have become so distorted that you are losing sleep over them, it is time at least to begin to think about leaving. Such a decision is never easy and should be approached prudently, with a great deal of thought, because you could end up leaving to work for another company that is even worse.

Whistle-Blowing: The Case of Special Agent Rowley

Whistle-blowers, depending on the circumstances, tend to be regarded with either admiration or contempt, and sometimes with a mixture of both. If they have "gone public" about a matter of safety or security, such as falsifying inspection reports of products vital to defense (e.g., batteries for missiles), burying memoranda indicating that a particular product is dangerous (e.g., certain motor vehicles), or misrepresenting toxicity levels (e.g., carcinogenic chemicals), whistle-blowers are usually regarded, at least to some extent, as heroes. If their reports have to do with matters less vital (e.g., fraudulent advertising), most of us are somewhat less ready to greet their actions with applause. The issue turns on how much indignation we feel about the alleged misconduct.

At least two reasons underlie our natural ambivalence toward whistle-blowing, one psychosocial and the other practical. The practical reason is that most people assume, naively I think, that if a person does not like what is going on in a particular organization, he or she always has the option to quit. This assumption is naive because, in leaving the organization, the whistle-blower often has to leave behind the core of a career. If one is, say, a professor of chemistry, the change may come to little more than an inconvenience, since the core of one's career may be a list of publications, for example, books and articles in professional journals. It is sometimes not all that big a deal to move from one university to another. If, by contrast, one has worked for a traditional company for fifteen or twenty years, one's career may largely consist of whatever reputation and goodwill one has been able to build up within that company. And so, leaving it for other employment sometimes results in a major career setback. Another reason the "you can always walk" argument breaks down is that in many instances there is no alternative organization to which one can move. This would likely be the case if one worked for the Federal Bureau of Investigation (FBI) or any other unique arm of government. Recall that a large percentage of our workforce does, in fact, work in the public sector.

The psychosocial reason behind our ambivalence toward whistle-blowing and whistle-blowers is more salient. Loyalty is a key value throughout most of the Western world, especially in the United States and Britain. People who blow the whistle on their employers tend to be perceived as betrayers and occasionally as "rats," "finks," or "stool pigeons." If we work for an organization that may suffer because of their actions, we feel all the more as if such people are attacking our "tribes" and, by implication, the affiliations that most powerfully define our social identities. And in a sense they are, since for a great many people in the modern industrial world, the entities for which they work are their *only* tribal affiliations.

It can be difficult to get the average person, who by definition has an IQ of 100, to understand that someone filing a valid report of improper corporate conduct is often demonstrating loyalty of a higher sort, namely, to society instead of to one's career or financial well-being. There will, of course, always be malcontent and paranoid individuals who, usually frivolously, often maliciously, and sometimes ridiculously, attempt to "blow the whistle" because they feel underappreciated, underpromoted, and undercompensated. Corporate attorneys may tell you that it is increasingly common for employees who are fired for poor performance to claim they were terminated for whistle-blowing. But when a solid citizen subordinates loyalty to an employer to loyalty to the public at large, at obvious personal price, it is an ethical act to be greatly admired.

Few whistle-blowing incidents in America have received as much attention as the one involving Coleen Rowley. On May 21, 2002, Special Agent Rowley of the Federal Bureau of Investigation wrote a thirteen-page letter to FBI Director Robert Mueller about the Bureau's repeated failure to act on information from the field office in Minneapolis. This information might have prevented some, perhaps even all, of the damage inflicted by terrorists on September 11, 2001. Because thousands of civilians died in those attacks, American citizens have been keenly interested in the United States' ability to detect and prevent such attacks in the future. They are also interested in why the government was unable to prevent what happened in New York. These interests turned Rowley into something of a celebrity on Capitol Hill and beyond, a role to which she did not seem to take naturally.

In her letter, an edited version of which appeared in the June 3, 2002 issue of *Time,* she stressed the crippling effects of bureaucracy within the FBI (too many levels of approval needed before action can be taken), how agents are punished more readily for mistakes than for risk aversion and inaction (which may have proved tragic in this instance), and the perverse results of "careerism" (which, citing *Webster's Dictionary,* she defined as "the policy or practice of advancing one's career often at the cost of one's integrity"). The FBI's Minneapolis chief division counsel, Rowley has been with the FBI—her "dream job"—for twenty-one years, and a division legal adviser for twelve. Valedictorian of her class, this razor-sharp attorney, mother of four, and "sole breadwinner of a family of six" is no slouch. Neither does she appear to be a troublemaker ("I have never written to an FBI Director in my life before on any topic") or a fool ("Although I would hope it is not necessary, I . . . wish to take advantage of the federal 'Whistleblower Protection' provisions by so characterizing my remarks").

I have studied her letter carefully and, before proceeding, want to emphasize that I have the highest regard for the FBI and have no desire to add to the bashing that it received in the wake of Rowley's letter. The FBI needs support more than it does criticism. Based on the contents of her letter, however, it also seems clear that major reforms need to be made in the interests of increased organizational agility. It is of no small significance that, responding in part to the legendary lack of cooperation among various intelligence agencies in the United States, President George W. Bush took the extraordinary step of announcing his intention to house the Central Intelligence Agency (CIA) and the FBI under one umbrella.[2]

The richness of the Rowley episode mandates that it be addressed in any discussion of ethics and whistle-blowing. Her letter seems to have been leaked to the press, and I suspect that she had nothing to do with the leak, but this is of secondary concern. Of primary concern is what one ought to do if and when one finds oneself in a similar situation.

Here are some guidelines that I hope will help:

1. Make every effort you can to resolve the problem informally. Special Agent Rowley appears to have done this. Whistle-blowing should be a last resort.
2. Ask yourself if you have what it takes to withstand the hostile attacks that blowing the whistle often entails. It is important to count the costs and to be realistic about them. Whistle-blowing is not a game for the faint-hearted.
3. Consult an attorney before—not after—you do anything that even remotely resembles whistle-blowing, because once you file a report, you cannot take it back, and it is likely to change your life forever.
4. Can you live with yourself if you do nothing? Special Agent Rowley seems to have decided that she could not. She had too much outrage.

When I was a teenager, I wanted to go to military school, and so, at the age of fourteen, off I went to a boarding military academy. As a senior, I was a high-ranking cadet officer who made it clear that I was serious about enforcing the institution's honor code. This did not endear me to some of my classmates, but I was voted the "most respected" member of our graduating class.

Fortunately, I never had to make the kind of agonizing decision that Coleen Rowley did. I never reported another cadet for cheating and, frankly, I don't know if I would have. Turning another person in to the "authorities" is pleasant only if you have a masochistic need to be castigated by some, ostracized by many, and second-guessed by all.

But sometimes it has to be done.

The Psychodynamics of Misconduct

Before ending this chapter, which to this point has been about pressures from others and where to draw the line, I want to discuss a few of the internal (psychological) processes that tend to get people in serious trouble.

Nearly all embezzlers, if and when they own up to their crime, will tell you how they believed the company "owed it to them." Whatever they embezzled, in their mind they deserved, since they were simply rectifying an injustice. This is also a common psychological attribute of those who commit treason. It is common for traitorous intelligence officers to turn out to have been people who thought of themselves as gifted but insufficiently appreciated. In their minds, they never advanced up the career ladder as they should have. And so they, too, were simply "putting things right"—as one of John le Carré's fictional spies might have stated.

When people work in one organization for a long time, they have a tendency to blur the distinction between themselves and the enterprise. This is not surprising, given what we said above about tribes and identities, but it can be dangerous. It is important, therefore, to keep the following reality in mind.

There is a clear distinction between your property and the company's. These are not the same, from paper clips on up. Be especially carefully about the common tendency to rationalize, "They were going to throw this away anyway, so I might as well take it home." However common such practices may be—and they are—stealing pencils is the beginning of a slippery slope that can lead to walking off with computers.

Notes

1. James C. Collins and Jerry I. Porras, *Built to Last: Successful Habits of Visionary Companies* (New York: HarperCollins, 1994).
2. The issue of communication among the various intelligence agencies is more complex than most people realize. When the CIA was created in 1947, for example, it was prohibited from both law enforcement and domestic operations, in part because President Harry Truman did not want it to become "Gestapo-like." This concern inadvertently discouraged the sharing of information between agencies and, in many cases, actually made it illegal.

4

Simple versus Complex Conflicts

Two Major Types of Conflicts

Ethical dilemmas often arise on short notice. Life will be moving along smoothly when, suddenly, you have to make a gut-wrenching decision with serious long-term consequences. What makes many moral decisions so incredibly agonizing is their sheer complexity, coupled with not knowing how to approach them, for example, how quickly to determine what's relevant and what's not.

Most formal codes of ethics are of little or no help in the face of such complexities, in large part because real-life ethical challenges involve trade-offs that, by their nature, cannot be resolved by consulting a list of do-and-don't rules, regardless of how well-thought-out or carefully crafted. Formal codes prove most helpful in clarifying what institutions regard as acceptable versus unacceptable personal/professional conduct, with heavy emphasis on the latter: "Thou shalt not." They are often minimally helpful when you have to decide which is the lesser of two evils—and such dilemmas and decisions arise frequently.

To give us a way to sort out some of the complexities and, in the process, to make what I write more concretely applicable and intuitively meaningful, I propose that we think of ethical conflicts as belonging to one of two basic types. The distinction to be made is between what I call *simple* and *complex* ethical dilemmas.

Simple Dilemmas

A simple dilemma is one that, in some sense, involves a relatively straightforward question of right and wrong. Calling the dilemma "simple" does not mean that the decision of what to do will, in every case, be easy or painless. But most of the time our fear of punishment, if nothing else, will be enough to keep us on the straight and narrow. Yet as human beings we face temptations in abundance, and even the best among us can falter in minor ways (we don't like to admit this, but it is nonetheless true).

Right-wrong or good-bad tensions—an ethical challenge or problem would hardly qualify as a dilemma without at least some tension—can take many forms, such as the violation of a law or some other formalized principle (e.g., a corporate code of conduct):

> *Example 4.1.* You are the mayor of a small town. An influential local businessman, a prominent land developer, offers to contribute money to your upcoming reelection campaign, which is badly in need of money. He "likes your stand on important issues," he says, and writes out a check, casually mentioning that he has filed a proposal for a new shopping mall with the planning commission and that he "would appreciate anything you can do to help." As it happens, you genuinely believe that a new shopping mall would greatly benefit the town, and it is highly likely that his proposal will pass, since it appears to be well reasoned and supported by solid environmental impact studies. Your opponent for mayor is a scoundrel who, in your view, wouldn't be fit to serve as dogcatcher, lest he sell the dogs as food to the boa constrictor merchant in the next town, but the election promises to be very close.

As with the other examples in this section, I will defer analyzing them until later. But, I do want to point out that laws, as discussed earlier, are typically put in place to protect society, that is, people in general. When an existing law applies to a particular circumstance, one had better have an awfully good reason to break it in the name of virtue.

British philosopher Thomas Hobbes (1588–1679) was born about three months premature because, as he was inclined to say, his mother, like the rest of England, was plunged into abject terror when she received news that the so-called invincible Spanish Armada was lying off their southern coast. It may have been this awareness, more than anything else, that prompted the personally genteel Hobbes later to argue that, without strongly enforced laws, life would quickly become "solitary, poor, nasty, brutish and short." The temptation to break a law usually involves the promise of being able to place one's individual or corporate welfare (specific outcome) ahead of society's (general outcome). As noted earlier, acts that are illegal are also generally regarded as unethical, although debatable exceptions exist.

Example 4.2. You are in charge of choosing the location for a large off-site meeting to be held for the top 147 management people in your company. The conference will run from dinner on Wednesday to lunch on Friday and will, therefore, require two overnight stays for everyone and many meals. Your CEO has made it clear that he wants this important event to be "flawless" and to "tick like a Swiss clock in the town square." The pressure to perform is on, but you have plenty of time to explore alternatives, since the conference is not scheduled to take place for three months. You arrange to visit the only three hotels in your area that can accommodate the meeting. At the second one you visit, the catering director says, "You will be dazzled by the excellence of our accommodations, the quality of our cuisine, and the attentiveness of our entire staff. And to prove it, I want you and your family to stay with us for a couple of nights. You will be my guest, all expenses paid, including meals and spa services, which I am sure you'll want to make available to those attending your event, or at least to their spouses."

This vignette is rich in material for analysis but, again, we defer this for now.

Example 4.3. You want to hire a person born and educated in another country, but when you state this to your immediate supervisor, he winces, scowls, and barks, "What are you thinking? We don't need any of *them* around here!" It is obvious that the candidate you want to employ is head and shoulders above anyone else who has applied for the position. And you didn't need anyone to tell you about the benefits of "diversity" to sensitize you to the stupidity, not to mention the evils, of xenophobia (fear of strangers). Nor does anyone, now, have to explain how much it could injure your future with the company to cross your supervisor.

This dilemma pits your values, judgment about what is best for the organization, and perhaps also your view of yourself as a fair and open person against your desire for personal career success and, perhaps by implication, the welfare of loved ones who may rely on you as a provider. To the extent this last assertion is true, I suppose you could regard this as a complex ethical dilemma (see below). But the major conflict here is between doing what is right and what is, in some sense, personally advantageous—not always an easy choice.

As in the two previous examples, a formalized (published) code of conduct will probably let you know what is right if you take the trouble to consult it and, even if you don't, your basic instincts and intuitions will probably (but are not guaranteed to) serve you well. You may nevertheless choose to do what you believe to be unethical, perhaps because you deem the price of doing otherwise to be too steep; but you will at least be able to discern the difference. With most of the nitty-gritty ethical dilemmas we face in our work life, neither formal codes nor instincts and intuitions are likely to reveal, in any unequivocal way, which of several paths we might trod is the noblest.

With ethical conflicts that do not involve the violation of a formal code, whether civil or corporate, the question often becomes "What sort of person do I want to be?" If, for example, I commit adultery, I define myself as one kind of person and, if I don't, perhaps as another. Such existential challenges have to do with one's self-concept, what psychoanalysts call one's "ego ideal," and, often, what many would consider to be basic ethical principles.

Sometimes a dilemma has little to do with your definition of yourself. But it may have a great deal to do with prudence, and perhaps also with observing an organization's code of conduct. The following seemingly simple but in reality subtle dilemma was brought to my attention by Brian L. Chew.

> *Example 4.4.* You are the pension fund manager for a medium-sized company, responsible for investing $600 million. The question before you is whether to invest up to 10 percent of these funds—$60 million—in your company's stock. If you do this, the price of the stock will probably increase.

Complex Dilemmas

Many of the ethical challenges that come our way force us to choose between two or more evils or two or more goods, which is what I mean by a complex moral dilemma. Although in its original usage the word *dilemma* had to do with circumstances in which there were only two alternatives, usage over the centuries has broadened it to mean "a problem involving a difficult choice," with the implication that facing this choice is unpleasant.

Self versus Other(s): How Much Do I Take Care of Myself?

> *Example 4.5.* A coworker has been assigned to do a project that could have important implications for her career. It soon becomes obvious that she is going down the wrong path and that, unless she redirects her efforts soon, she will not only miss the deadline but deliver an inferior product as well. If you enlighten her, she is almost certain to ask for your assistance with the project, which to do well will be time-

consuming, and you already have more to do than you can comfortably handle. Two further complications are that (*a*) she has been known to get nasty with those who refuse to assist her and (*b*) both of you are candidates to replace your current supervisor, who is scheduled to retire within the year.

Example 4.6. You own a real estate company that specializes in helping to site new supermarkets. For twelve years you have located, purchased, and then resold properties—usually large vacant lots situated on corners—to a certain national chain, with the result that the chain acquires prime locations at a favorable price and your firm makes a healthy profit. The director of market development retires from the chain, and you learn that his successor, a bright and ambitious up-and-comer, is thinking about cutting your company out of the loop. You know that the chain intends to build a new store at a certain intersection in a rural town, and you have drafted a preliminary offer to buy one of the corner lots at this intersection—the only intersection that would prove suitable for the new store. A friend tells you one afternoon that the new director is about to purchase one of the other corners, all four of which are for sale. You can tie up all three in escrow if you move quickly to buy them (with appropriate off-ramps in the offers, so that you can back out), which would force the chain to continue to do business with you.

Self versus Institution, Group, or Organization: How Much Do I Take Care of Them?

Example 4.7. You manage a department that is responsible for providing three kinds of services for your company. Your boss informs you, in confidence, that one of these services will be "outsourced" in three months and the employees who currently provide it internally will be let go, but that you cannot share this information with anyone else, including your subordinates who will be affected. One of these subordinates comes to see you a week later, seeking career advice. She is a single mother with three young children. Her ex-husband is a flake who has left the state, so she is getting neither alimony nor child support. She is clearly living on a thin margin, from paycheck to paycheck, and says that she has been offered a job at another company. Because that job pays slightly less than the one she holds, her preference is to remain where she is, working for you. "Does the company have any plans to outsource my section?" she asks.

Self versus Society: How Much Do I Take Care of Civilization?

> *Example 4.8.* You are a police officer and know for a fact that a certain person recently mugged an elderly woman. The man who did it also broke your thumb five years ago when you attempted to arrest him for disturbing the peace. It has still not healed properly. The woman is in the hospital recovering from her injuries. The suspect has a long record of arrests and convictions for violent crimes, ranging from aggravated assault to armed robbery, and he was in prison until five weeks ago. Unfortunately, you have no usable (admissible) evidence to connect this obvious societal menace to the mugging. Another officer comes up with a clever way to arrest him for an unrelated crime (of which the suspect is probably innocent), which would almost certainly lead to a solid conviction.

Organization versus Organization:
How Much Do I Worry about Fair Play?

> *Example 4.9.* You are a marketing representative for a steel manufacturer. The dominant steel producer in your geographical area has just filed for bankruptcy, which has left several of its major customers stranded and therefore eager to enter into long-term agreements that will ensure them a reliable supply of steel. It is your job to land as many of these potentially lucrative contracts as possible. Based on current market prices, coupled with their terror at the prospect of being left without adequate supplies, potential customers are willing to buy your company's steel for X dollars per ton. You have information about some pending advances in technology that will radically bring down the price of steel in a few months. If you disclose this information, potential customers will insist on a price substantially below X, which will deprive your company of revenues it desperately needs to survive. If you do not disclose the information and the contracts are signed for X, you will surely end up with some very angry customers. Your boss is counting on you to close these deals and, if you don't, your company, too, may have to seek the protection of a bankruptcy court.

Person versus Person: Whom Do I Choose?

Here is a dilemma that is close to home for a lot of management people these days. It is at least in some sense a "tragic moral choice," insofar as whatever you do is likely to involve some element of the tragic. If you want to understand how horrible such choices can become, read William Styron's *Sophie's Choice*—or rent the movie.

Example 4.10. The company is reorganizing and, in the future there will be only one job in claims administration whereas up until now there have been two. Two men, both in their forties with large families, are currently working as claims administrators. Both can do the job, but neither is especially talented, and you therefore doubt that whichever one you put on the street will be able to find a comparable job. There is no other position in the company for which either man is qualified, and neither is old enough to qualify for retirement. The one you let go is going to have a hard time of it, and so will his wife and children.

These are but a few examples, yet they should at least get you thinking about how nasty ethical decisions can become—and how difficult they may be to make.

In the next two chapters, we will explore some ways of approaching them.

5

Guidelines for Survival

In this chapter I will present some simple guidelines for staying out of trouble when you confront what I have termed simple ethical dilemmas. When I label such dilemmas "simple," I do *not* mean that deciding what to do in the face of them is always simple. If it were, there would be no need for this chapter. As explained in the previous chapter, I mean by a "simple ethical dilemma" one that revolves around a dichotomous choice—do it or don't do it—and one in which there is some established code that bears directly on your decision.

Types of Conduct Codes

This code may be quite explicit, as in laws that govern the operation of ordinary motor vehicles by private citizens on public roads. While you and a police officer may debate whether or not you entered the intersection when the light was red, there will be little or no discussion about what the law mandates. Or the code may be fraught with ambiguities and require considerable thought for its proper interpretation and application. Many corporate codes of conduct are of this nature.

To the extent that a particular code is *principial* (concerned with and consisting of abstract principles) rather than *transactional* (concerned with and consisting of concrete behaviors), it is likely to prove difficult to apply. While for this reason it is desirable to strive for making such codes transactional, sometimes the best you can do is to remain at the principial level, as we will see poignantly in our discussion of "conflict of interest."

Some trade-off between breadth and precision will probably always exist. The more abstract the standard or principle, the more broadly it can be applied, which of course requires judgment and at least some capacity to think conceptually. The more concrete the standard or principle, the more easily it will be applied, albeit probably more narrowly.

Getting Clear about the Issues

Decisions are often easier to make if you understand the issues involved—what's at stake. And even then, you may struggle. As I will demonstrate, these issues are not always straightforward or transparent. Sometimes you have to think long and hard about the circumstances, alternatives, and potential implications before you even notice that an ethical issue exists.

General Approach to Simple Ethical Dilemmas

Whenever you face what you consider to be a simple ethical dilemma that you find difficult to resolve, there are two things you should do immediately if possible:

Consult knowledgeable and wise colleagues. Perhaps the single best thing you can do is to consult others. These should be people whose judgment you trust and, ideally, those who know something about the area in which you have to make a decision. If you have any concerns whatsoever about the legality of the act—especially if you are thinking about doing it—talk with an attorney. This is important because lawyers will often see critical issues and problems that others do not. If you ever find yourself in trouble, one of the sweetest things any attorney representing you can hear is that, before you did whatever it is that you're accused of, you consulted with colleagues, preferably "expert" colleagues.

Consult whatever codes of conduct apply. You may not always know what codes of conduct bear on the decision you have to make, so consult others whenever you are unsure. All of us are subject to the laws of the land. Hence, if we violate a provision of the criminal code, we can be prosecuted. If you work for a large organization, it probably has some kind of a code of conduct, and if you violate that, you may be terminated. And if you are a member of a profession, you will be subject to its ethical standards.

A certified public accountant (CPA) who works for a traditional corporation therefore will be subject to at least three codes: (1) all federal, state, and local laws; (2) the company's published code of conduct; and, (3) the ethical principles of the American Institute of Certified Public Accountants. Depending on what he or she is actually doing, additional standards of conduct may also apply.

Screens and Filters

I want to highlight some of the more important areas for you to consider when you confront a simple ethical dilemma. These areas are by no means the only ones and, in a particular situation, they may be far less important than some not addressed here. They do, however, reflect the sorts of things one typically has to be concerned with; they are the ones often highlighted in corporate codes of conduct.

Federal, State, and Local Laws

The first question to ask is whether you will violate a law—and, if you are unsure, ask a lawyer. In Example 4.1, it does not matter one iota that your opponent in the mayor's race is a scoundrel. Nor does it matter that you think the land developer's proposal is wonderful or that it is "highly likely" to pass without your help. It seems reasonably clear that he is attempting to influence you, and bribing a public official is a crime. So is accepting a bribe if you are a public official.

Many specialized laws may apply to you, depending on the nature of the work that you do, and to the extent that this is true you should familiarize yourself with them. These may include the Foreign Corrupt Practices Act, the Export Control Act, and—if you work in defense—even the International Traffic in Arms Regulation, which governs the sharing of certain kinds of defense-related technologies. They may also include injunctions against doing things that inhibit competition, such as fixing prices or predatory pricing.

Conflicts of Interest

It is obvious to most people that they cannot violate federal, state, or local laws without risk; this risk is usually enough to keep them from doing so. Avoiding conflicts of interest is another matter, however, in part because it is sometimes difficult to see them coming. The potential for such conflicts to arise is almost limitless, and if there is any one concept that I would like to get across in the first part of this book, it is the importance of being able to recognize and avoid them.

Consider Example 4.2. What's the harm in accepting the catering director's offer? The problem is that it could easily cloud your judgment when you have to decide which facility to use. In the example, the consequences of failing are high, since the CEO wants the conference to "tick like a Swiss clock." You may conclude, therefore, that accepting the catering director's offer—spending the time at the property—would be all the more desirable. But it can be argued that this is actually a reason for *not* accepting the offer. What makes this example particularly interesting is that most people who have the job of arranging meetings may, in their own corporation's eyes, have a duty to try out the various facilities, to ensure that they are up to snuff. In an ideal world, the corporation would pay the full tariff, rather than relying on freebies.

Example 4.4 is even more interesting, because it involves a potential conflict that is not obvious. If, as a pension fund manager, you invest in your company's stock, the price of its stock is likely to rise, which in itself seems like a good thing. If you sell such a large amount of stock sometime in the future, however, the stock price is likely to decline. Suppose at some future time the company is not performing as well as expected and its stock price goes down. Your duty, as a fiduciary of the pension fund, may be to start unloading it. But if you do, this may accelerate a further decline in the price, which in turn could even precipitate a massive sell-off, for example, by large institutional investors. None of this is going to go down well with your senior executives, whose job performance evaluation by the board of directors, not to speak of their compensation, will likely be linked to price per share. By purchasing shares of your company's stock for the pension fund, you are potentially creating for yourself a condition of divided loyalties. You are supposed to do what's best for those whose well-being is affected by the well-being of the pension fund. As you execute these responsibilities, it is not a good idea to put yourself in a position where you have to think about the overall well-being of your enterprise (its value as reflected in price per share), the goodwill of senior officers and, by implication, your own hide. Another example of a conflict would be your financial planner recommending that you invest in a company in which he or she has a financial interest. Some people think that it is also suggestive of a conflict when a financial planner recommends that you buy a "product" whose sale yields the planner a commission.

Before leaving the subject of conflicts of interest, I want to point out two other things about them. The first is their close relationship to what are customarily called "dual-role relationships." Each role we play in life carries with it expectations, responsibilities, and so on, and these can easily conflict. This is among the reasons that family businesses can be so difficult to operate, and also why they often become vitriolic. Even in the most open and tolerant of working environments, one's subordinate—someone you pay to carry out the duties you assign—has only a limited capacity to resist, object, argue or, in the extreme, say no. But what if your spouse is also your subordinate? Spouses are not usually inclined to demonstrate the same level of deference as a non-related subordinate.

Entering into financial partnerships with one's subordinates creates two potentially conflicting sets of expectations: one revolves around the (hierarchical) axis of boss-subordinate, and the other revolves around the (egalitarian) axis of comrades in a joint venture. It's all fine, on the surface, when things are going well. Partnerships, however, are notoriously difficult to make work, so this sort of dual-role relationship is an invitation to trouble. So is becoming romantically involved with someone who works for you. How can you give orders to your lover, who is likely to feel demeaned by such conduct?

The other point—and it is an extremely important one—is how the law presumes that no one is able to withstand a conflict of interest. While many conflicts of interest are not illegal, such as the ones outlined in the previous paragraph, some are. And when they are, their mere existence is enough to get you into trouble. Suppose, for example, you are a U.S. senator who owns ten thousand shares of an oil company. Suppose, further, that you have to vote on some measure that could affect the profits of this company. It will do you no good whatsoever, after you cast your vote, to claim that you were not influenced by the securities in your portfolio. The odds are that you will either be severely censured (if you get off easy) or criminally indicted.

Beware of gifts. Accept no gratuities. Refuse amenities and accommodations unless it is eminently clear that no one would construe you as having a "consequential relationship" with the other person or entity. Anything that tempts you is probably bad. If it's free, watch out. And anything that places someone else in a conflict of interest is ordinarily regarded by companies as bad practice. Although there are unscrupulous persons and enterprises that intentionally create such conflicts, they should be avoided. Deal straight up or don't deal at all.

If you're going to act counter to this advice, at least know who you're dealing with, recognizing that pleas about this person's good character, or your own, will do you no good if anyone accuses you of a conflict. A wonderful rule to live by is to avoid even the *appearance* of evil.

Violations of Conscience

Example 4.3 is difficult because it forces you to choose between your well-being and what you know to be right. Federal statutes prohibit discrimination. And if your company's code of conduct is anything like most others, it too expressly forbids it. This is certainly an instance of potential discrimination and, if you simply go along, you will be participating in it. In the wake of recent events, we could make this example even more interesting by assuming that the person you want to hire is from a country that may be harboring terrorists.

You could discuss the matter with someone from your Human Resources Department, and some experts on the matter might advise you to do so. No matter what you do, if you are "on the way up," you will probably be thrown into conflict. We talked in Chapter 3 about the value of peremptory decision making, suggesting that it may make sense to decide in advance what you will and will not go along with. This sort of thing may be on your peremptory "no-way" list. Then again, it may not be, and you may cave in to the pressure.

You have to decide what kind of a person you want to be. If you do not think about this consciously, circumstances may decide for you, which I would argue is not a good thing. There is a lot of talk these days about "defining moments." The best defining moments are the ones that you have with yourself, in the privacy of your own mind; the ones when you decide what is, and what is not, acceptable for you as a human being.

Information Management

A good many of us have to deal, in one way or another, with sensitive or confidential information, and often there are subtleties involved. One subtlety is the difference between confidentiality and privilege, and what happens to the latter when you behave injudiciously. Confidentiality is a standard of conduct and, in the case of a psychologist for example, it is a serious ethical principle. Privilege, by contrast, has to do with the ability of a court of law to gain access to certain kinds of information. Whatever you tell someone who is functioning as your attorney (e.g., a member of your company's law department who is advising you on a business matter) is ordinarily privileged and, if anyone tries to get at it in a legal proceeding, the attorney will "assert the privilege." Courts will usually honor such assertions. But if it can be demonstrated that you disclosed this information, say to the waiter in the corporate dining room casually during lunch one day, the privilege has been forfeited. If you work in certain industries, losing the privilege can be a grievous act of negligence.

At the most basic level, all organizations expect their employees to protect their intellectual property, including copyrighted materials. Proprietary information, such as trade secrets, company records, nonpublic documents, employee information, and market intelligence, typically cannot be shared outside the enterprise. Organizations also expect employees not to *use* company information for personal gain or for the gain of persons close to them (e.g., family members).

Violence and Threats of Violence

Most corporate codes of conduct are quite clear about overt violence and prescribe specific actions that should be taken if, for example, an employee hits another employee or brings a firearm to work. But the situation sometimes becomes ambiguous, and hence more difficult, when the person is engaging in behavior that others believe but are not sure is threatening. If you encounter such a situation, it is important that you not stick your head in the sand and hope the problem goes away. One option is to consult with the Law Department, if your organization has one. If you work for a company with a written code of conduct, check it to determine what action it prescribes. Usually this action will be to contact "Security," if such a department exists, or to notify Human Resources. This can be tricky and, regardless of what you do, there is likely to be at least some risk—risk if you act and risk if you do not. Again, the main idea is to get consultation from responsible parties as quickly as you can without being indiscreet or defaming anyone (e.g., saying that someone is "violent" when there is no evidence of this).

Potential Embarrassments

Another question to ask yourself is whether your conduct could prove embarrassing to you or your organization. A practical test is to ask yourself how you and those with whom you work would feel if tomorrow you were to read in the newspapers a full report of your actions. If whatever it is you're thinking about doing would fail this newspaper test, you probably shouldn't do it. Another version of this is the sleep test. If your actions are likely to keep you awake at night, be careful.

Gyroscopic Wobbling

Throughout most of my life, I have found it useful to pay special attention to my intuitions. One metaphor I use for this is a gyroscope. When things do not feel right, it is almost as if an invisible gyroscope inside me starts to wobble, perhaps because I feel like I'm losing my balance. Regardless of what you call it, you, too, have an inner gyroscope. Pay careful attention to it, because it is likely to prove itself a good friend.

Is this gyroscope an infallible guide? No, it isn't; which is why, when in doubt, you should consult others around you who have wisdom to share.

6

Complex Ethical Problems

I t can be useful to view complex ethical dilemmas in terms of what duties we owe to whom and the damage that is likely to be done if we breach these duties. Another way to say this is that we can examine complex ethical dilemmas through the lens of a personal liability suit, the elements of which I outline below. An attorney could do a better job of elucidating the finer points and nuances of such a suit, but our interest here is not legal elegance as much as practical utility. The basics I present will, I think, be sufficient for our purposes.

Before going into what society customarily defines as personal liability, I want to reiterate what I mean by a complex ethical dilemma. It is one in which you have to choose between at least two competing goods or two competing evils. Often the options open to you are mutually exclusive: if you do A, you cannot also do B. In practice, the choice is frequently between several or even many alternatives or between various sets of pluses and minuses—hence the awesome difficulty that often attends real-world ethical problems.

Elements of Personal Liability

For personal liability to exist, the following conditions must be fulfilled:

1. There must be a duty owed to another person or entity. Personal liability suits can be brought only by someone with a "standing to sue"; you cannot, for example, sue someone for injuring another person with whom you have no connection, say because you read about his or her

injuries in the newspapers. So, the first question to ask yourself is this: *To whom (e.g., individuals, groups, or organizations) do I owe duties?*

2. The duty or duties owed must be breached, that is, the person(s) or entity (e.g., corporation) owing the duty must fail to carry it out. Whether or not such a failure occurred in a personal liability litigation is typically determined by comparing what was done or not done to the standard(s) of performance ("standard of care") operative (i.e., prevalent) in the community. What has been expected of a physician attempting to serve people in a rural area, for instance, has traditionally been less than what would have been expected of the same doctor if he or she had been practicing in a large urban area. Such differences in the "relevant community" are becoming less important all the time; the standard against which a doctor is measured is increasingly becoming national rather than regional. Here is the second question to ask yourself: *What would a reasonable person of ordinary prudence, working in a comparable organization, do in this or a similar situation?*

3. Damage has to be done to the person(s) or entity to whom or which duties are owed. In a personal liability suit, the damage is to the "plaintiff," the person or entity bringing the action. Regardless of what anyone feels, no liability has been created—at least not that the courts care about—if there has been no damage. The third question, then, is this: *Could specific injury occur, and to whom, and if so how serious might it be?* Courts are ordinarily concerned only with damages to which a monetary value can be attached, but as suggested below there can be damages that are difficult to translate into dollars.

4. By failing to carry out the duty, the person owing this duty has to be the legal ("proximate") cause of the injury. This is the issue on which a good deal of liability litigation turns—it is the "element" of suits on which everything else turns. There may be multiple persons or entities responsible, in one way or another, for the damage. So the fourth question to ask yourself is this: *By failing to perform my duty, will I be the cause of whatever damage is done?*

These, in a nutshell, are the sorts of questions you might want to pose. I have outlined them in a streamlined fashion so that they will be easy to use, but I want now to comment on some of them in more detail.

Comments on the Elements

Some ethicists assert that, in any action with ethical implications, there is always a duty owed to *all* of humanity. The German philosopher Immanuel Kant

(1724–1804), for example, advised that when confronting any ethical choice, one should choose as if one's decision were to become a universal standard.

The phrase "reasonable person or ordinary prudence" is a legal term of art. Such a person is, of course, an imaginary construction, in part because it is impossible to know for sure what anyone else would do in the "same or like situation," much less to know what a mythical person would do. Still, it is a useful concept. What would others generally expect of me? What might *they* do if faced with my dilemma? In analyzing ethical dilemmas as if they were occasions for potential personal liability—which, when you think about it, they most certainly are—we are wondering what a person who is neither excessively scrupulous nor deficient in conscience would do. If such an average person were looking over my shoulder, what would he or she find acceptable conduct?

By defaulting on *this* duty will I be able, as a consequence, to fulfill a competing duty, say one that ranks higher in moral importance? How can I tell which duty is the more compelling? Answering that question has been among the principal concerns of philosophers through the ages. Will stealing a loaf of bread from a manor house allow me to feed my sick starving child who, perhaps aided by this modicum of nourishment, might be able to recover from an otherwise lethal pneumonia?

While it can be argued that one should do one's moral duty regardless of whether failing to do it will cause injury, when faced with ethical decisions in everyday life—concrete rather than abstract choices—we just about always "factor in" consequences. And when we have to choose between two or more alternatives, each of which is complex and carries with it a different set of possible or certain consequences, we are forced to rely on calculations about outcomes—whether we like it or not.

Sometimes what, as ordinary and casual observers, we would interpret as causation may be viewed differently in the courts, and occasionally such technicalities allow the person who may, in our judgment, be morally responsible to "get away with it." But such niceties of legal analysis are largely, if not entirely, irrelevant to ethical dilemmas, for at least two reasons.

First, if we approach ethical choices with any integrity whatever, we are not going to spend time and energy searching for loopholes, ways to weasel out of our moral responsibilities. Sure, we might have moments of rationalization; but if we're sincerely interested in ethics, we will, by definition, be concerned with doing the right thing. Sociopaths, who major in rationalization and the discovery of loopholes, have never been known for their attention to questions of right and wrong. The mere fact that you are reading this book suggests strongly that you are not a sociopath.

Second, the law is appropriately concerned with redressing wrongs that have already occurred, whereas ethical reflection has mostly to do with preventing, or at least minimizing, wrongs before they happen. The ethically sensitive person wants to know what injuries he or she might inflict, so that he or she can minimize these "in the aggregate." How best to achieve such overall ("net") minimization is the core concern of many (but not all) professional ethicists.

The question of determining the true and total "costs" (i.e., damages) to injured parties—especially determining these in advance—is rarely straightforward or easy to answer because, unlike courts of law, the person of principle will be concerned with a lot more than money. In addition to possible economic injuries, he or she will think about and attempt to anticipate psychological ones. What, he or she will ask, are likely to be the emotional costs? Will there be subtle social costs, such as loss of status or diminished reputation? How about political costs, for example, "standing" with others in the company, whether peers or superiors? And what about upward mobility, in the case of an individual, or "brand equity," in the case of a product or service provider such as a particular department? Even at their best, courts find it difficult, if not impossible, to detect and affix monetary value to all of these. An ethically concerned person will do his or her best to take them all, and perhaps much more, into account when someone else's welfare is on the line.

Analysis of the Examples

In the interest of demonstrating how challenging complex ethical decisions can be to make, I want to comment on the remaining cases in Chapter 4. It is not my intention to tell you what to do in these examples. I have opinions about some of them but am less certain about what I might do in others. The principal reason for including the examples in this book at all is to give you a chance to build up your ethical reasoning muscles.

Example 4.5. The consequences of helping your coworker, who is also a competitor, appear to be predictable, so the main issue is whether you want to extend yourself. One way to decide this is to ask what you would want her, or indeed anyone else, to do in your shoes. According to the facts presented, you are already overloaded and, thus, if you have a family at home, whatever help you give her is likely to keep you from them.

Example 4.6. There are practical issues here. If you tie up all the available real estate, you will very likely make the new director of market development furious with you, and this may make it likely that you will do no further business with the supermarket chain—certainly not while this person holds the position. The ethical issue has to do with whether or not to enter into contracts to buy properties that you have no intention of buying. Unless I intended to compensate the owners of the other three properties for their time and inconvenience, I would not offer to buy their properties under these conditions. And even if I did compensate them, I would clearly be deceiving them. Some, of course, might argue that that's the way the game is played in real estate, and this may be so.

Example 4.7. If she asks whether you think she should take the other job, you might say something like "It's always good to have more than one company on your résumé," thus indirectly encouraging her to accept it. But this does not get you out of the jam, because your supervisor probably wants her to remain for the next several months, and subtly encouraging her to leave is violating the spirit, if not the letter, of this desire. If the subordinate asks you the point-blank question printed at the end of the example, the best you may be able to do is to say something along the lines of "It wouldn't be appropriate for me to discuss plans for possible outsourcing with you now." Anyone who could fog a mirror might conclude from this that the answer to the question is yes. Thus you would still be violating the duty that your supervisor imposed on you. An interesting question is whether it was proper for your boss to impose this duty, that is, to give you this information while instructing you not to share it. This sort of thing is done all the time in companies and may even be necessary for them to run well.

Example 4.8. I don't know for sure what I would do if I were the policeman in this instance, but the analysis seems relatively straightforward. With my heart, I want to send the sleazy mugger up the river, maybe for life. But with my head, I know that we shouldn't do it that way because, once we start down the path of falsifying evidence, where do we stop? If the people who are supposed to uphold the law begin to break it in the interest of justice, we are going to have problems as a society. This is partly why, during the investigations into the scandals surrounding Richard Nixon, it was so often stated that "no one is above the law"—not even the president of the United States. On a more mundane level, it is also the theme behind some of Clint Eastwood's films, in particular *Magnum Force*, in which police officers were executing criminals who had either "beat the rap" or avoided prosecution altogether. This example raises the issue of to what extent ends can be used to justify means.

Example 4.9. This case is worthy of considerable discussion. You might point out to your boss that it makes little sense to alienate a customer for life in the interests of posting a short-term score. But what, in the real world, is likely to be the case? In a fast-moving industry, your boss may not care. Nailing down those multiyear contracts may be far more important to him or her. If so, you would be caught in a nasty bind between pleasing your boss and doing your duty to your company on the one hand—remember our mention of the duty to protect market intelligence in Chapter 5?—and being an open human being who negotiates with candor on the other.

Example 4.10. I have no easy answers here. It almost seems as if you could toss a coin. In the real world, which is what we've been talking about all through this book, such decisions may be quite difficult to make, and you may agonize. In the end, there is perhaps not much point to agonizing. You could, of course, try your best to find one of the two men a job elsewhere but, with the time constraints most of us are under, the chances of your doing this, or doing it successfully, are small.

The World of the Philosopher

A philosopher who specializes in ethics is likely to be concerned with whether people accept responsibility for the implications of their actions and is also likely to point out that, in order to do so, they must understand what these implications are. The philosopher may also press for a set of internally consistent (i.e., noncontradictory) rules according to which ethical decisions may be made.

Normative ethics help people make decisions. The substance of normative ethical systems can be seen, therefore, as a set of rules or procedures for evaluating the relative merits of alternative options.

Although there are many approaches to making ethical decisions, these approaches are usually sorted into two broad categories: theories that focus on duties and those that focus on consequences. Duty-based ("deontological") theories—theories of intention—specify the intrinsic nature of what we should do, while consequence-oriented ("teleological") theories specify that "for the sake of which" we ought to do this or that.

It is not our purpose here to discuss any of this in detail. I simply want to indicate that these theories exist, in case you have an interest in exploring them, and to highlight the two key questions that you might want to ask yourself when you face ethical dilemmas:

1. What is the nature of my duty or duties?
2. What are the likely consequences of choosing the various alternatives open to me?

We turn now to some of the world's most respected literature on prudent conduct: the book of Proverbs.

PART II

Ancient Wisdom for Modern Times

Introduction to Part II

Author's note: Although I have never met Bob Wentworth, I asked him to write a brief here's-how-it-works-for-me introduction to this section. Prior to joining the Environmental Safety Division at the University of Georgia, Dr. Wentworth was with the federal government's Centers for Disease Control and Prevention.

When Clinton McLemore's *Good Guys Finish First* hit the shelves in 1983, America was awash in how-to books on success. The usual recipe? Some combination of intimidation, manipulation, and corner cutting: take every advantage you can and let the other person worry about ethics. It was the age of the ruthless.

Our society is again learning the hard and painful lesson that, when such thinking becomes the norm, the costs can be staggering—costs that are making headlines every day. Investors, large and small, hurt by questionable business and accounting practices. Broken relationships, stemming in part from a "me-first" approach to life that says, "my way, today, or it's over." Children growing up with too little guidance, as their parents struggle for fame and fortune, which takes precious time and attention away from these children who occasionally shock us with their violence.

Over the past two decades, I've reached countless times for my now yellowed and battered copy of *Good Guys Finish First*. And, last year, when I was interviewed by our University Communications News Bureau and asked for the book that I would most recommend to others, I cited this one. More than anything else I've read, these fifty short chapters—here revised and updated—highlight the limitless value of human relationships, business or personal, and the ability of ego, laziness, or pride to damage and derail them. The author's main point, never stated explicitly in these chapters but implicit in every line, is the importance of character.

This section of *Street-Smart Ethics* has the potential to revolutionize not only one's career but, more broadly, one's life. Open to any page at random and the truth jumps out: we benefit by being people of integrity. Whether or not all "good guys" succeed in their careers, the application of the principles in this book will lead to more ethically appropriate business decisions, healthier social institutions, and stronger families. Far more than a set of strategies for success in business, this is a prescription for a better world. It is a call to decency. This book belongs in the hands of every corporate leader, every spouse, and every parent.

ROBERT W. WENTWORTH, PH.D.
UNIVERSITY OF GEORGIA

How to Get the Most from This Section

S treet-Smart Ethics is, in large part, a guide to staying out of trouble. Whether you work for a large corporation, a small business, or "for yourself," whether as an executive or an entrepreneur, secretary or salesperson, it is intended to be a handbook to take with you into the trenches.

The fifty principles I am about to discuss will, I hope, serve as both a survival guide and prescription for success. Everything in this book rests on the assumption that doing well in life is desirable, that surviving and thriving are inherently good, and that there is no intrinsic merit to suffering, failing, or ending up behind the proverbial eight ball.

If you have evil goals, attaining them will do no one any good, and if you are a monster of a person, your very survival may not even count for much. But, I am not writing for monstrous people with sinister motives. This book is for people who want to better themselves and who are willing to put some serious effort into doing so, those who are willing to do what it takes. My purpose, in this section, is to provide you with some high-leverage information that you can use to stay out of trouble, ethical and otherwise.

Western society, on the whole, seems to have progressed beyond the crassness of "looking out for number one" and "winning by intimidation," themes that were rampant throughout many sectors of our society twenty and thirty years ago. Those trends were what led to the writing of such books as Christopher Lasch's *Culture of Narcissism* (1979; revised edition, 1991). At the same time, human beings will always be self-interested—some, of course, more than others—and, so, we will always experience temptations and the conflicts that come with them. Among the best ways of coping with such temptations is to prevent them from developing in the first place. To do this, however, requires considerable savvy. Where might we look for such enlightenment?

Throughout the history of civilization, certain people have been specially gifted with practical wisdom. They knew what to do. Fortunately for us, some of their thinking has been preserved in written documents, which makes it possible for us to learn from them. We can read how various sages of the past thought about practical dilemmas and, so, absorb and benefit from their insights.

This, of course, is the great value of books, whether set down on papyrus, printed on paper, or transmitted electronically. The invention of writing allowed information to be stored, in a more or less permanent form, outside the human brain. Reading a book amounts to learning what is, or was, in another person's mind. Pouring through the musings of great thinkers, whether alive or dead, can be like listening to them talk. If we could read with our eyes closed—and, in a sense, we can if someone else reads to us—it would not be difficult to imagine ourselves sitting at Socrates' feet, conversing with Confucius, or walking around Galilee with Jesus.

If one had to choose the book that most reflects the wisdom of our civilization, of its roots and heritage, it would have to be the Bible. Written over the course of about a thousand years, the Bible is actually a collection of over sixty books. Its three quarters of a million words span a critical period in the formation of civilization: from when people were nomads, trying to establish a stable society, to when humanity began confronting, with sophistication, the key philosophical questions of human existence. The Bible, therefore, gives us a series of historical portraits, including graphic descriptions of what some very discerning people came to understand about how to survive and succeed.

Of the books contained within the Bible, Proverbs is most explicitly concerned with concrete advice, with actually telling us what to do. Many of the individual proverbs, or wise sayings, are probably King Solomon's, who as much as anyone in history is remembered for his sagacity. We even use the word "Solomonic" to refer to someone who is wise. Solomon, you may recall, was the ruler who divined which of two women was the true mother of an infant by ordering the child to be cut in two: the true mother, in a desperate effort to avert tragedy, begged Solomon to give her child to the impostor.

Other proverbs represent the wisdom of persons whose names have long been lost. Who they were remains a mystery. What scholars have always agreed on, however, is that Proverbs is a most extraordinary book that seems as relevant today as it did thousands of years ago. This section of *Street-Smart Ethics* represents my best attempt to unpack fifty of the most pithy and strategic sayings in the book of Proverbs. They are pithy in the sense of being highly substantive and strategic in that they embody definite strategies for survival and success.

Proverbs is a kind of textbook, intended to instruct. It specifies how to prosper, how to stay out of trouble, and how to handle difficult people. On the other hand, Proverbs is not arranged in the way that contemporary texts are—carefully organized, each point following from the last, lots of illustrations, and so forth. To the twenty-first-century reader, it sometimes appears to be a disorganized collection of unrelated truisms, a mere hodgepodge. This, however, it is not. Neither is it an atlas of cheap and clever tricks for taking advantage of others.

However jumbled up Proverbs may seem to the casual reader, it points relentlessly to the fundamental tendency for goodness and prosperity to go together. This is the universal principle glaringly missing in many self-help books. Bad people do occasionally prosper—as stories like *The Godfather* suggest—and good people do occasionally lose. Nevertheless, it remains true that graciousness and integrity, coupled with the right measure of prudence, are tremendous personal assets. "Nice guys finish last" is often an excuse for personal failure or, worse, a thinly veiled justification for ruthlessness.

At the same time, it has been correctly observed that if you are honest because "honesty is the best policy"—because it brings you rewards—your honesty is flawed. If you have made it this far in *Street-Smart Ethics*, it is probably because you have an interest in doing the right thing for its own sake, not just because it may benefit you.

We live in a world of instant this and instant that. Yet, few worthwhile things come to us without effort. To get the most out of this book, carry it around with you and, when you get a few spare moments, take it out and read a little of it. Familiarity is the key to profiting from the proverbs in this section. You will probably have to go over them, until they become part of you, since you will draw more from these ancient lessons if you immerse yourself thoroughly in them. But, how can one best do this?

Based on some well-established principles from the psychology of learning, here are some suggestions:

First, quickly go through this entire section—all fifty proverbs—to get an overview of what it contains. You can skim it in a half-hour or, if you prefer, breeze through the material in one or two sittings. This kind of initial survey will give you some intellectual hooks on which to hang ideas as they occur to you later. Time spent in this way will yield substantial dividends.

Second, select the one subsection from the ten that most interests you and read through it carefully. Then, in a few days or a week, read the same subsection again. Repetition is essential to internalization. Research has demonstrated that you are likely to learn better if what you are trying to remember is emotionally meaningful, which is why I recommend starting with what most interests you, and not necessarily at the beginning of Part II.

Third, read through the remaining nine subsections, one at a time. A helpful approach might be to alternate between subsections that strongly interest you and ones you find less engaging. You will soon get to the point where you only have to read the proverbs, since you will remember most of what is contained in the accompanying commentaries. On the other hand, few of us may so thoroughly internalize the proverbs themselves that we will never again have to read them. *Street-Smart Ethics* should, therefore, be a book that you can use for many years.

Keep in mind that "spaced practice" is better than "massed practice." It is usually better to study one hour today and one hour tomorrow, for example, than two hours back to back on either day. Naturally, there are exceptions, times when studying all at once is best. Find out what suits your personal rhythm of learning.

Read actively. As much as possible, I have encouraged such reading by posing questions about how the guidelines might apply to your life. Take this even further if you can. Again, the more emotionally meaningful, the better you will remember the material, and the easiest way to make anything emotionally meaningful is to relate it to yourself.

Question everything:
"Is that true?"
"Do I buy it?"
"When have I observed this sort of thing happening in my life?"
"In other people's lives?"
"Are there times when the opposite seems to be true?"

Write your personal reactions and comments in the book as a way to interact with it and, thus, make it more alive.

All of this takes more energy than casual reading, but the effort you invest will yield wonderful results. Challenge, reflect, apply. The more, the better.

Finally, keep a record of how many times you study each guideline. You can do this in a number of ways, but probably the easiest way is to put a check next to a guideline each time you work with it. Such elementary record keeping will give you a real sense of accomplishment and suggest where you may need to put most of your efforts in the future.

I sincerely hope that, as you make your way through what can be the dense jungles of modern life, these proverbs and comments will prove to be a steadfast ally—a reliable friend, a source of inspiration, and a trustworthy companion, there to assist you at a moment's notice.

Note on Bible translations: In the citations from the book of Proverbs, the number before the colon indicates the chapter, while the number after the colon refers to the verse within the chapter. Thus, "2:14" stands for the fourteenth verse in the second chapter. If a verse contains two parts, the letters "a" and "b" stand, respectively, for the first and second parts of that verse. Initials are used to designate specific translations, as follows: JB = *Jerusalem Bible*; NEB = *New English Bible*; NIV = New International Version; NJB = *New Jerusalem Bible*; NLT = New Living Translation; NRSV = New Revised Standard Version; REB = Revised English Bible; RSV = Revised Standard Version; and TLB = *The Living Bible*.

Fundamental Graciousness

GUIDELINE 1: The tongue has power of life and death; make friends with it and enjoy its fruits (18:21, REB).

"Your brother Harry, of course, has always been smarter than you."

"Well, it's just your personality. You know. You're just not . . ."

"Look, buddy. I don't care whether you're the boss or not. I think you're a jerk!"

In this age of fierce competition, the value of simple graciousness is often underestimated. Yet, as nearly all etiquette books point out, basic decency underlies many of our social customs. At the root of good manners is a heartfelt concern for the other person.

The most important aspect of manners, good or bad, is what we say. Accordingly, Guideline 1 highlights the awesome power of the tongue. As this ancient saying indicates, people have died because of what they or others said or failed to say. Words are powerful. They can build and give life. They can tear down and destroy. It is usually easier to destroy, however, than to create.

Proverbs contains a whole series of sayings about loose or otherwise improper talk, and we examine them in some detail later. For now, let us simply note the emphasis that the writer of this particular proverb places on making friends with our tongue. It is as if the tongue were an unruly relative with which we are forced to live. There is no choice but to calm and, if necessary, subdue it. Once tamed, the tongue becomes a wonderful tool that will yield bountiful fruit on our behalf.

Misled by amateur self-help psychology, some people believe that the best way to ensure success is to bully others. "Speak up. Don't let yourself be walked on. Let 'em have it! Demand what you want." Such strategies may occasionally have their place, and they will certainly get you what you want in certain situations. But they can be lethal to long-term relationships, whether at home or in the office. Many promising executives have been permanently promoted "down the hall," where no one ever saw them again, simply because they were rude or careless in what they said. These once-rising "stars" did not understand the tremendous power of words.

I once watched a door-to-door salesman use his tongue to intimidate potential buyers. They almost always bought something the first time he came around, but from then on he could never find them at home. They were chronically "out." Such can be the result of callous self-assertion.

Most successful people, especially those with major executive responsibilities, are far more smooth than abrasive. They artfully craft what they say, knowing how important this is to their effectiveness. They realize, in the words of another proverb (16:24, NEB), "Kind words are like dripping honey." It is of great relevance that a number of recent large and well-done studies of executive attributes have revealed that self-control, what is sometimes called "self-regulation" by those who study emotional intelligence, is the key distinguishing characteristic of high-performing CEOs—not intelligence, not strategic vision, not even technical competence or the willingness to work fourteen hours a day, all of which are pretty much threshold conditions. To survive as the CEO of a large company, you have to be smart, possess the ability to envision the future, know how to transform your enterprise from vision into reality, have sufficient knowledge of your industry to be able to sift the wheat from the chaff, and have an enormous capacity for work. But, by themselves, these attributes, however wonderful, will not make you a great CEO. You also have to be able to restrain your impulses to criticize, blurt out the "answer" to a problem (which, even if ridiculous, will be celebrated by sycophantic staffers as the greatest of wisdoms, to the detriment of you and the business), and make other people feel inferior or insignificant. When the chairman—who is often also the chief executive officer—spits, the basement floods.

None of this is intended to be a justification for manipulation. As we shall see, a central theme of Proverbs is the wisdom of avoiding all forms of treachery and deceit, which often come back to haunt us. These sayings simply remind us of the immense power of verbal communication. Words, though they may seem unreal because they are invisible, can be strikingly real in their effects.

Over forty years ago, sociologists casually spread the rumor in a small town that its only bank was shaky and about to collapse, more or less proving how beliefs that are real are real in their consequences. The bank, which had been quite solid, came close to faltering because its depositors, frightened by the specter of insolvency, began to withdraw funds at an accelerating rate. It was like a scene out of the Jimmy Stewart film *It's a Wonderful Life*. Words can indeed have powerful effects.

People who justify (rationalize) their verbal insensitivity in the name of candor are fooling themselves. What they attempt to dignify or excuse by invoking the term *honesty* others regard as boorishness. Verbal brutality is socially ineffective and often self-destructive. Cut others with the lash of your tongue and, when they can, they will usually try to get even.

Build them up with sincere words of affirmation and support, however, and they will love, appreciate, and reward you. The next time you are tempted to "let someone have it," count the potential costs. There are certainly times to assert yourself, but reckless confrontation is by definition a foolhardy tactic.

Questions for Reflection

Is there someone at this moment whom you are tempted to tell off?

Might there be a better way to accomplish your objective?

Is there someone you ought to build up with your words?

GUIDELINE 2: He who conceals another's offense seeks his goodwill, but he who harps on something breaks up friendship (17:9, NEB).

Most of us have a strong tendency to relish the sensational. For complex psychological reasons, we like the shocking, the scandalous, even the sordid. In the business world, where competition prevails, our lust for the sensational can prove overpowering, since the other person's blunders and mishaps often make us look all the better by comparison.

"Did you hear what Johnson did?"

"Remember the Miller account? Well, Barton just lost it!"

"That's not my fault. Harrison's the one who didn't get the stuff in on time."

A successful acquaintance of mine once developed such a reputation for business savvy that many young executives would go to him when they needed advice. Often they asked general questions about how to "make it" in what they perceived—with some justification—as shark-infested waters. Because he was such a seasoned warrior of corporate combat, who, in his words, had gotten "a lot of blood on his own shirt," his advice tended to astonish them: "Make the other guy the hero."

Such advice is contrary to a lot of how-to-succeed-in-business counsel, which often advises us to engineer our own grandeur. If there's any chance they're going to hand out swords to fall on, make sure the person next to you is viewed as a more worthy recipient.

The business relationship in which loyalty is most important is the one with your boss. Make the boss look good. Don't detract from his or her prestige by claiming credit for everything you do. Serve!

Recall Aesop's fable about the lion and the mouse. As the story goes, a mouse finds herself caught under one of the huge paws of the lion. "Please," begs the mouse, "let me go and someday I may be able to repay you." Reluctantly, and only after scoffing at the absurdity of a small creature ever being able to help such a majestic and ferocious beast as he, the lion complies. Some time later, the lion becomes hopelessly ensnared in a hunter's net. The mouse appears and, by chewing through the ropes, repays the lion's earlier benevolence.

When someone around us is vulnerable, we temporarily become the lion and therefore have a golden opportunity to be merciful. It is important to remember that, in the fast-moving world of business, roles can quickly switch, and often do. Today's mouse may be tomorrow's lion, and vice versa. Your subordinate today may become your boss tomorrow.

In advising us to conceal others' offenses, the author of this proverb is not advocating perjury or martyrdom. He is recommending kindness, saying, in essence, "Don't opportunistically make a big deal out of someone else's blunder. Facilitate the other person's glory. Work for the other person's good." By advertising others' frailties, you tend unnecessarily to lose friends and allies, and in business, such losses can prove lethal. Lose enough allies and you may lose your job. Even if you own the company, you may alienate valuable employees or forfeit valuable accounts. Always remember the enormous value of framing what others do in the best possible light.

Questions for Reflection

Whose "offenses" or failings might you be able to minimize?

Is there anyone you can help to become a hero?

GUIDELINE 3: It is to a man's honor if he avoids quarrels, but fools never exercise self-control (20:3, JB).

Imagine that you are asked to gather some information, perhaps related to an important job that your company has to do. You conscientiously collect it, meticulously arrange it for presentation, and deliver your finished product. There is no question in your mind that you have done your duty with distinction and that absolutely no one else could have done it any better.

Now, suppose that, after all this, someone viciously attacks the work you have done. Your critic calls it "incomplete," which most certainly it is not, as well as "sloppy" and "superficial." Beyond this, after spending many extra hours on the project, for which you will not receive one extra penny of compensation, you are even accused of being "lazy." What would your reaction be?

Many people at this point would blow up. It would not matter if the critic were the president, a coworker, or the firm's best customer; there would be a violent reaction. Instead of remaining cool, they would find it necessary to defend their honor.

An acquaintance of mine has an index card posted on his bedroom mirror. On it are typed the words "You are not the target!" This is a difficult concept to keep in mind when someone is maligning you or your work. It is hard not to take such insults personally. However, refusing to personalize irrational attacks is, in fact, what effective leaders are able to do. Contrary to widespread opinion, most successful businesspeople are not combative. They know better.

Let me add, as an aside, that the best corporate players—good street fighters—might also choose not to respond immediately to outrageous and unjust criticism. They would "forgive and remember." Regardless of how things may seem at the moment, your worst antagonists may *not* be out to get you. People sometimes attack the person nearest to them, or simply the person who seems least likely or able to retaliate. However unfair, this happens a great deal in life. The issue is whether such unfairness can hook you, draw you into a senseless battle.

The eminent psychiatrist Karen Horney pointed to the dangers of what she called "neurotic pride." Something can be said to be "neurotic" when, even though it does not work (e.g., does not get us the security and self-esteem we want), we do it over and over again. She noted that almost all of us maintain an idealized conception of ourselves that, if challenged, leads to a sense of outrage, a feeling of "How dare they!" Some people, for example, fly into a rage if anyone questions their integrity. Others start swinging if their "manhood" or "dignity" is threatened. The more neurotic pride we harbor, the more inflexible our behavior becomes.

A major difference between humans and animals is that our behavior is potentially more versatile, more adaptive, more responsive to the circumstances in which we find ourselves. Interestingly, the New English Bible translates the second half of Guideline 3 as "it is the fool who bares his teeth," and the Revised English Bible puts it as "every fool comes to blows." People in many parts of the world telegraph their aggressive intentions by exposing, and sometimes clenching, their teeth. This is also what large primates do, which is why it is not always a good idea to smile at gorillas, especially if they are close enough to grab you. The author of this proverb is telling us to act flexibly, as human beings, not reflexively like apes.

The trouble with reflexive aggression is that, with it, you can add fuel to an already explosive mixture. Interpersonal combustion can occur rapidly and, before you know it, you are caught up in a terrible blaze. Most murders occur not on the streets but in the kitchen or bedroom. Few people who have committed such a murder ever saw it coming. Like the protagonist in Albert Camus's *The Stranger*, we can easily become the victims of bizarre circumstance, with the result that our lives can be radically and permanently changed.

Whenever you possibly can, back away from hostile disputes, so that you do not become the unwitting target of someone else's self-defeating behaviors. Maintain your poise. Retain your flexibility. No macho stuff. No getting hooked.

Questions for Reflection

What sorts of criticisms or challenges tend to embroil you in senseless arguments?

What can you do to avoid such arguments?

What tends to push the buttons of your pride?

GUIDELINE 4: To answer a question before you have heard it out is both stupid and insulting (18:13, REB).

"Let's get on with it." This is what I am usually thinking when I answer someone's question before I've fully heard it. Occasionally, I finish the question, answer it, and then discover that I've answered the wrong question.

Most of us are extremely time conscious. We treat time as a precious commodity whose value is lost unless we efficiently invest it. Because productivity is customarily defined as "output per unit time," work tends to be one endless game of "Beat the Clock," which makes us all the more time conscious.

Unfortunately, Beat the Clock can be lethal. Medical psychologists have established that certain personality characteristics tend to be associated with coronary disease, perhaps because they foster hypertension (i.e., high blood pressure). These Type A traits include competitiveness and the tendency to rush. They also include the tendency to talk too much, to the point that one physician who specializes in stress-related diseases suggests that Type A people would live a lot longer if they simply stopped talking. Thus the "stupidity" to which the proverb writer refers may be more than social. Finishing other people's questions may be a sign that we are also finishing off ourselves. The author of this proverb is commenting on a general frame of mind. He is warning us against hyperactivity.

Cutting off other people is fundamentally disrespectful. It tells them that we care more about the information they have, or about the information that we think we have, than we do about them and what they may need to express.

Although people rarely say it, they almost always feel punished when some-one else cuts them off. Underneath the momentum of any conversation in which one person is pushing the other is likely to be some resentment. We all want to be listened to, to feel that what we have to say is important.

People vary in their temperaments, however, and therefore some of us are more impatient than others. There are strong biological contributions to these temperament differences. Even newborn babies show wide variations in their activity levels. Some are slow and easy, while others are jumpy and tense. Adults show similar differences.

If you are one of the "fast" people, as I am, you will probably have trouble letting slow people communicate at their own rate. Always you will want to hurry them along. Yet it is important to realize that many people who speak slowly think quickly. Speech rate is not an index of intelligence. So, even aside from the disrespect of adding your words to someone else's question, pushing them may cause you to miss important information.

Graciousness is a great aid to wisdom. By listening patiently, you can pen-etrate more deeply into issues. Careful reflection almost always triumphs, sooner or later, over flashy wit and quick conversation. Moreover, by surren-dering to time pressure—the pressure to get on with it—you can easily spiral yourself down into a pit of anxiety. Sometimes the more you rush, the more you feel the need to rush. You let your psychological center of gravity get out-side yourself and then spend the rest of the day trying to recapture it.

Earlier I mentioned how a wealth of research is suggesting that impulse control is an important quality in a CEO. The same research is revealing some-thing else that runs completely counter to conventional business wisdom. Among the attributes most highly valued by employers has been "sense of urgency." In evaluating executive candidates, for example, it has been tradi-tional to focus on how much they felt driven to get things done quickly. It turns out that what is called, in the current literature, "pace setting" is not a desir-able attribute in a chief executive and, indeed, it may even be detrimental because the rush to get things done yesterday often goes along with a relative absence of prudent reflection.

Professional interviewers have also discovered something that runs counter to natural expectations: communication often becomes more effective as it becomes less focused. In other words, more information will be exchanged if people can communicate what and how they want to. Naturally, if you want a specific answer, you need a specific question, such as "When will you turn in your next budget?" Most of the time, however, for both parties effectiveness of communication goes up as freedom of expression increases.

Try this experiment: Make an effort to let others finish their questions. Force yourself to wait three seconds after they finish talking before you begin.

This may be hard to do, but I think you will like the resulting peace of mind, which is probably not what you feel when you rush in with answers.

In my thirties, not long after I began working as a management consultant, the president of a large company said, "It would be better if you waited longer before answering. I know that you're smart and that what you would say later may not be much different than what you might say now. But answering so fast makes it seem like you aren't taking the question seriously, as if you're trivializing it." I tried after that to take a deep breath, wait a little while, and give the other person plenty of time to say whatever it was that he or she wanted to say. Do I still have that Type A tendency to rush in? Sure. But over the years I've gotten better about this, and so can you.

No human beings on earth are generally as winsome as those who are truly interested in what you have to say.

Questions for Reflection

Whose questions do you most often finish?

How much does each of these people like you?

Are you satisfied with your own style?

GUIDELINE 5: A gift opens the way for the giver and ushers him into the presence of the great (18:16, NIV).

A gift given in secret soothes anger (21:14a, NIV).

Suppose you wanted to meet an eminent person. How would you go about it?

If you were fortunate enough to know someone who knew the eminent person, you might simply ask your acquaintance to give you an introduction. But suppose you were not so fortunate. You could try sending a gift.

Before proceeding further in this discussion, I want to make clear that many times the giving of a gift is either inappropriate, unethical, or patently illegal. The U.S. Foreign Corrupt Practices Act, for example, forbids companies domiciled in the United States to give gifts in order to secure business in other countries. That some American corporations operate at the margins of this law does not change things. It is still illegal for American companies to pay bribes to get business. Our discussion here assumes that there are no ethical or legal injunctions against the giving of a gift to the intended recipient.

Gifts have tremendous symbolic value. They tend to be loaded with meaning, perhaps because we long to return to childhood when we were given presents as expressions of adult love. The best gifts are probably those that have the most symbolic value to the persons receiving them. Such value is not always reflected in a high price tag.

Suppose you knew that the person you wanted to meet was raised in India and collected miniature elephants. A few hours rummaging through resale shops could turn up something inexpensive that he or she might treasure.

Even a note of appreciation will, in some circumstances, prove to be a wonderful "gift." I have repeatedly found that writing sincere notes of appreciation to eminent people almost always makes them more receptive to a personal conversation or visit.

The proverb writer is not recommending insincerity. As we shall see, many proverbs, such as the second half of 2:14, soundly renounce flattery and other forms of deceit. He or she is simply advising us to express our goodwill tangibly.

Consider another situation. Suppose someone were angry with you and you wanted to assuage his or her anger. You could, of course, simply apologize. Apologies do not always work, however, partly because "words are cheap" and partly because trying to talk with angry people sometimes only augments their fury. Again, you could quietly give a gift. You might, for example, have something sent that you know the person would like—a radio, a book, a basket of goodies, flowers, whatever. The note attached might say nothing other than that the gift is from you. The other person might remain angry, but at the very least you would probably throw him or her off balance for a moment, in a constructive manner.

People who are angry usually feel, at root, frustrated and helpless. We tend to get angry at anything that threatens to cause injury. When people are angry with us, they typically feel that we have somehow cheated them. Giving gifts to such people can restore their sense of being treated fairly, which of course can calm them and increase their happiness. Friends do this sort of thing all the time. Wherever one of two good friends has been neglectful, for example, he or she will more readily agree to something the other wants—a kind of gift giving.

The catch is that you have to give the gift without fanfare. Otherwise the angry person is likely to feel awkward or embarrassed and, as a result, become even angrier. Your good intentions will be rewarded only with pain. You have to make sure that the gift is more or less casual, that it does not cause any loss of face, any sense of being patronized or babied.

Remember that gifts are symbols of appreciation and esteem, and that symbols are carriers of implicit meaning. If you make symbols too explicit, they lose their value. Hence "I am giving you this nice gift to cool you off" is not likely to prove effective.

It is usually difficult to give to someone who is angry with us. That person's anger tends to put us on the defensive, even to kindle our own anger. This is precisely the time to give, to soften, to do the unexpected.

Some small investments yield huge dividends, and the giving of gifts can be like that.

Questions for Reflection

To whom in your life might you wisely give a tastefully chosen gift?

Whose anger might you soothe with a present?

GUIDELINE 6: Withhold from no one a favour due to him when you have the power to grant it (3:27, REB).

It is sometimes hard to bring ourselves to repay certain kinds of debts. Most people pay their bills on time, partly because they know that their credit ratings will be impaired if they do not. But it is sometimes harder to work up the motivation to return favors. Knowing that this time it is our turn to pay the check, do we not on occasion go to lunch with certain people only reluctantly?

Almost all human transactions, especially in business, rest on trust. Every time you write a check or hand someone a charge card, you are asking that person or business to trust you. Every time someone accepts such promissory items, he or she is agreeing to grant you this trust. Even the gas or electric company supplies energy to your residence only because its directors believe that you will pay for what you use. Democracy itself is ultimately based on such trust and would not function long without it. If most people did not believe that the "system" worked, however blemished by inequities, there would be anarchy.

To refuse to pay a debt is shortsighted opportunism. You may win in the short run, but in the end, everybody loses. Society cannot run on breached contracts. Most everyday contracts involve the exchange of promises. To break a promise is to forfeit your honor. The breach of a small promise results in the loss of a little honor, while the breach of a large promise results in the loss of a lot of honor. Even if no one brings the matter to your attention, your trustworthiness will from that point forward be at issue.

Sometimes our responsibilities for payment are subtle. If, for example, other people work for you, there is always at least an implicit understanding that you will reward them for carrying out their duties, and that you will reward them even more if they do so with distinction. There may be no written or oral contract. You may never have announced any kind of special bonus for those who do well. Nevertheless, it is an unspoken assumption in business that the worthy will be rewarded in accordance with their worthiness. As another translation of this proverb states, "Do not withhold good from those to whom it is due, when it is in your power to do it" (NRSV).

There are, of course, many kinds of rewards. Money is the most visible reward, but there is also promotion, appreciation, and recognition. The good manager is one who knows which reward to give and when. A friend of mine once wrote a book in which he suggested that there are at least eight "languages of love." There is the giving of presents, the verbal expression of affection, the physical demonstration of love, and so forth. Good lovers tailor their choice of language to the needs and desires of the other person. Sometimes a word of praise is far more effective than the most lavish trinket. As in love, so in business.

"Jan, thank you. Thanks for staying late and typing all that stuff."

"Sandy, I appreciate the time off you gave me last week. Is there something extra I can do to help?"

"Dave, there's only one thing wrong with this article we're publishing together. You deserve to be the senior author."

To withhold what you owe someone else is, in essence, to steal. It is also to slight. People will not remain loyal to you if you steal from or slight them. They will feel ripped off and resentful, and often they will not mention it. How you treat your personal debts, tangible and intangible, speaks volumes.

Try to ensure that others see you as trustworthy and honorable, as worthy of their loyalty and affection. Since few of us fulfill all our social responsibilities, making a deliberate effort to do so will enhance your standing as a person and as a leader. People will like you, respect you, and regard you as a true friend.

One of my very close friends, the former CEO of a large company for which I have consulted for many years, is known for his high sense of ethics and the frequency with which he writes personal notes of affirmation and appreciation to others. The two, it seems to me, are somehow connected. And he wrote the notes as often, if not more, when he was a chief executive officer and, by implication, tremendously busy.

Questions for Reflection

To whom, if anyone, do you owe a debt or a favor?

To whom can you grant a "good" that is deserved?

GUIDELINE 7: An open rebuke is better than hidden love! (27:5, NLT).

A woman I know once worked for another man who, unfortunately, could not bring himself to say anything nice to another person, including his subordinates. The man was a good person whom I liked but who, like most of us, was less than perfect. He did not know how to give "strokes," even little ones, and the effectiveness of his leadership was substantially impaired as a result.

Neither did he seem fully to grasp how much productivity his "hidden love" was losing him and the organization for which he worked. Many of his people spent their time wondering, worrying, and complaining, time they could better have spent working. A brief compliment to each of them, now and then, would have done wonders.

Some managers deliberately keep their subordinates off balance, on the theory that "keeping people anxious" improves their performance. Usually, it does the opposite. Industrial research seems clearly to indicate that frightening people increases productivity only when they are doing such monotonous tasks as piecework and when a supervisor can closely monitor their output. For the jobs that most of us do, whether these involve creating spreadsheets or filing folders, insecurity quickly impairs performance.

I once even heard a psychologist attempt to defend his aloof and withholding style by arguing that giving people less reinforcement makes them more productive. His reasoning was based on what is known as "the partial reinforcement effect." This is the principle that "organisms" will continue to do something longer, when the goodies stop, if these goodies have been delivered intermittently and, best of all, inconsistently. A rat that is fed only once in a while for pressing a bar will continue to press it longer when the food stops, for example, than a rat that is rewarded every time it presses. People, however, are not rats. Even if they were, bar pressing is very different from perusing budgets or coming up with creative marketing plans.

Managers who believe in emotionally starving their subordinates should read *The Prince*. This early-sixteenth-century classic, written by Niccolò Machiavelli, warns against ruling by fear and threat. Such management "works" only as long as you retain power. Lose it for even a little while and, since you have built up no affection for yourself in the hearts of those managed, they may tear you to bits.

All of this relates to what used to be known as Theory X and Theory Y. Subscribers to Theory X believe that people will do only what they are forced to do and only what you reward them for. Hence, you have to watch them all the time, lest they cheat. Subscribers to Theory Y believe that people are inherently trustworthy and that, given the opportunity, they will generally prove worthy of your trust.

Even assuming that the people around you do not fear you, they cannot live on your unexpressed appreciation. Everyone needs affirmation. Without it, they wither and start to act in strange and unproductive ways. Their attention turns away from their jobs, toward finding ways to meet their needs for validation.

To say "I value you even though I don't say it" is to present a very weak case. You may possess warehouses of wonderful food, all purchased with another person in mind, but if you do not share it, the other person could die of starvation. Generals engender the loyalty of their troops by making sure they are adequately provisioned. Managers need to do the same. And so do nonmanagers.

Some people know it is good to say warm things to others but cannot bring themselves to do it. If you have difficulty expressing positive feelings, admit it, at least to yourself, and do something about it. Start practicing. Begin with something easy, such as a simple "Thank you." See if you can work up to "I think you're a terrific human being!" Only make sure that you mean it!

Questions for Reflection

Toward whom should you express more appreciation?

Who in your life needs more affirmation—and might you provide it?

Some Necessary Caution

GUIDELINE 8: Good intelligence wins favour, but treachery leads to disaster (13:15, NEB).
The wise man sees evil coming and avoids it (14:16, JB).

"Don't cross the line," the writer of the first proverb seems to be saying. "Don't get too smart for your own good."

Before I became a management consultant, I practiced for twenty years as a part-time, and for two years a full-time, psychotherapist. Occasionally, I would find myself working with a truly brilliant person who used his or her brainpower for perverse ends. One boy I remember well was, by anyone's standards, extraordinarily intelligent. Unfortunately, for a number of his adolescent years he used his cortical endowment to mastermind thefts. Again and again he paid a stiff price for this misapplication of his giftedness.

Intelligence is a tool and sometimes a weapon. Applying intelligence without good judgment is like shooting at random on a crowded street, and using it for treachery is like assassination. The very people who hire them often despise assassins, and many assassins are themselves assassinated. Predators often end up as prey.

What exactly is intelligence? Although technical definitions vary, most include the idea that intelligence involves the capacity to learn and to reason. Another way to put this is that intelligence is the ability to acquire information and solve problems. It is also the capacity to adapt to changing circumstances. Intelligence is the talent for organizing and using knowledge.

Wisdom, by contrast, is the judicious application of knowledge to everyday affairs. A person may be able to do higher mathematics faster than anyone else and still not be wise. Such a person may continually allow himself or herself to be swindled or to jump from one bad relationship to another. Some relatively unintelligent people, however, are remarkably wise. They know how to live. What they know about arithmetic might not impress a bright fifth-grader, but they have insight—they are able to see—into practical matters and to make good decisions about them.

As the author of the second proverb suggests, a central attribute of the wise person is the avoidance of evil. This, of course, is the core message of this book. You cannot avoid what you do not see, so wisdom in this sense involves something akin to what we described above as intelligence. To see evil coming and still walk into its clutches has to be the quintessence of foolishness.

But what is evil, and exactly what is so dangerous about getting involved in it? Just as there has been much debate over the best definition of intelligence, great scholars have argued mightily over exactly how evil should be defined. Is evil a thing in itself, or is it merely the absence of good?

We will not try to resolve such issues here, except to state that often we use *evil* to mean a bad act that has the potential to do serious and unwarranted damage. One reason that the writers of various proverbs tells us that it is wise to avoid evil is that if we do not, there is a very good chance that we will eventually be counted among its victims. Those who live by the sword tend to die by it also.

I once knew someone who, in order to increase the profits of his already hugely successful business, threw in with some unsavory characters who, I suspect, were heavily involved in organized crime. He found himself in increasingly difficult predicaments, until eventually he lost control of a multimillion-dollar business that he had worked hard to build.

Evil is like heated tar: touch it and you get it all over you, attached to everything you do, everything you own, everything you stand for, even everything you think and feel. Plus, it tends to burn terribly.

Use your intelligence for good, and keep away from anything unsavory, whether treachery or another self-toxic activity.

And if you are currently stuck in the tar, choose a good adviser and begin the process of extricating yourself from it.

Questions for Reflection

With what particular kinds of intelligence are you most blessed?

How can you make the best use of these gifts?

What specific evils do you need to make sure you avoid?

GUIDELINE 9: Impatience runs into folly; advancement comes by careful thought (14:17, REB).

Suppose you are in a meeting and an important issue is raised for discussion. At some point, you want to influence the decision that has to be made. What should you say and when should you say it?

Ironically, the more you care about an issue, the more likely you are to speak prematurely. More times than I can count, I have rushed in when I should have waited. Clearly, if you wait too long to board the train, you'll be standing on the platform when it pulls away. If you board without thinking, however, you might end up on the wrong train or even sprawled out on the tracks. So much in life depends on timing and forethought.

An ex-colleague of mine had the habit of waiting until everyone else had said what they wanted before he would speak. He then gestured to the chairperson, sometimes by twitching his index finger. He was almost always immediately recognized. I was sure that if he were sitting in a fine New York restaurant, far away from the kitchen, and suddenly whispered for the chef, someone in a white hat would instantly appear. Once he was recognized, he waited about three seconds—they seemed like hours!—before he began to speak. By this time, everyone in the room was silent, hanging on his every word, waiting to hear his next utterance. Partly because of this well-practiced style, he was a very effective communicator.

Impulsiveness often leaves you looking, if not acting, silly. Trial attorneys understand this. They deliberately needle witnesses to get them upset. Once this happens, the credibility of these witnesses has been sharply reduced. The impression generated is usually this: "If this witness can't even keep cool under cross-examination, how could you possibly rely on anything he or she says? Why, this person is unstable." Such a conclusion may not be fair, but it does tend to be drawn by jurors.

"Careful thought" requires patience, the opposite of impulsiveness. Patience is, among other things, the ability to endure tension, to live with unpleasantness or uncertainty, instead of rushing in to end it. When we say or do things impulsively to reduce our discomfort, it almost always turns out badly.

Most accidents occur because someone fails to think before acting. Someone pulls out of a driveway without looking. Someone else changes lanes on the highway before making sure that it is safe to do so. And still another person decides, just this once, to take a chance that proves fatal. It is no different in business. Although once in a while an impulsive move may later show itself to have been rooted in sheer genius, such moves have ruined far more careers than they have enhanced.

Impatience is like a disease that, if untreated, gets worse. This is partly because of our ability to self-program. Software becomes firmware which, in turn, becomes hardware. It is also because doing something—almost any-thing—when you feel tense usually reduces your level of tension, which is pleasant ("reinforcing"). Doing anything that leads to the reduction of anxi-ety, therefore, makes it more likely for you to do it again. To end this self-perpetuating cycle, it is important to stop yourself from such escapism. Instead of scrambling to terminate your tensions, stay with them for a while. Get to know them. They occasionally turn out to be our closest friends.

By attending carefully to your inner emotional processes, you can begin to train yourself in the art of patience. You can, as it were, sneak up on yourself, on your proclivity to leap before looking. In the process you will actually be practicing careful thought.

Remember—from careful thought comes advancement, which an older translation renders as "distinction."

Questions for Reflection

Has diligent thinking helped you advance?

How much "distinction" do you enjoy because you are known for your careful thought?

What sorts of issues are most likely to prompt you to become impatient and thus push you into the realm of folly?

GUIDELINE 10: Be timid in business and come to beggary; be bold and make a fortune (11:16b, NEB).

Another translation of this verse, which appears only in the Greek (Septu-agint) version of the Old Testament, is "The timid become destitute, but the aggressive gain riches" (NRSV).

Patience and timidity are not the same thing. To be patient is to weigh alternatives until you know what you should say or do. To be timid is to be unable to act, frozen by fear, even after you know what to say or do. "Go for it," the proverb writer is urging. "Once you know what to do, proceed with-out vacillation."

What would you do if you had a business idea, say a new invention, which you were convinced could be extremely successful? Out of fear, would you procrastinate? Or would you take the risk of failing, which is often the only road to success?

A friend of mine, when he was in his late thirties, decided that he was finally going to do what he had always wanted to do: launch out on his own. Having worked as an engineer for many years designing automotive products, he had the training and experience to do this sort of creative work with great exper-tise. With his wife's support, he mortgaged their home and moved forward.

What he did, in fact, was place himself in a position where he had to succeed. There was no room left for timidity!

What happened is one of those great success-in-business stories. There is a reasonably good chance that you have owned a car that was equipped with one of his accessories.

Here's another story. A young man who went around with holes in his jeans took the LSAT (law school admission) and GMAT (business school admission) tests after graduating from college and ranked in the ninety-ninth percentile on both. His father told him that he could probably get into any law or business school in the country and added that, indeed, he should make application forthwith. "No, Dad," said the son, "I think I'll stick with computers. And, by the way, do you have any domain names you'd like to register?" You may be able to imagine the rest of the story. The son, now in his thirties, had the courage of his convictions and, as a result, became extremely successful. He went for it. Oh, by the way, I was the father.

If such stories make you envious, keep in mind that everyone has a different calling. You might not enjoy spending your life making and marketing automotive parts. And you might not have been cut out to become an Internet entrepreneur. But there is no doubt something you would enjoy. The critical question is whether or not you are doing it.

Let me emphasize that family men should not ordinarily drop everything they are doing, risk everything they have, and pursue imaginary money trees. Such behavior is not much different from risking your net worth at the racetrack. You might win briefly but, in the long run, you will probably go home with empty pockets. Many compulsive gamblers, who are usually people who end up borrowing or stealing money that they inevitably lose, were big winners the first time out. And like compulsive gamblers, some businesspeople do not know when to quit. If the deck is stacked against you, the time to quit is before you start. Many people have been ruined by infatuations with harebrained schemes.

Investment analysts are forever pointing out that good investors know when to sell. Part of the lore of Wall Street, for example, is "Good traders take their losses." If they have purchased a bad security, they get rid of it, even if they are behind. Most investors do not do this because they don't like losing. They tend to hang on to their bad stocks and sell off their good ones. So you have to be flexible and, as another friend of mine insists, stay unattached. If the venture is clearly bad, get out of it or, even better, never get into it in the first place.

The other side of this analysis, however, reads like this: Good investors are courageous. Not foolish, just venturesome. They willingly take risks when the conditions are promising. Sometimes they win and sometimes they lose, but they do not have to lecture themselves in the mirror for lacking initiative. Others tend to see them as having brains *and* guts.

I should add that all proverbs are generalizations. Hence, you cannot assume that boldness alone will guarantee prosperity. We need to balance the gambler's daring with the sage's circumspection. The goal is to have both prowess and prudence. As a legendary frontiersman put it, "Be sure you're right, then go ahead." By all means, do go ahead!

Questions for Reflection

At this point in your life and career, how would you evaluate your tolerance for risk taking?

Is there something you would like to accomplish that seems to be hindered mostly by timidity?

GUIDELINE 11: A king's threat is like a lion's roar; one who ignores it is his own worst enemy (20:2, NEB).

Some people are so "out of it" that they do not comprehend the most obvious dangers. Somehow, they just miss the fact that certain things or certain people can hurt them. But this proverb is really about something else—authority problems.

I worked for years as the chief psychologist for a vocational guidance center. During those years, I did a large number of psychological evaluations on people with career troubles. Many of them were in midlife and distressed over not having achieved what they had hoped. Sometimes they had been fired, sometimes just not promoted. Whatever the reason, they were attempting, with the center's help, to take a thoughtful look at themselves and, in many cases, they were edging toward, if not rushing into, a job change.

The information I obtained through the assessments often indicated that the client had trouble getting along with those in authority. Sometimes the person knew this, but often he or she didn't. The individual would simply rationalize (make excuses for) his or her inability to relate to superiors: "Oh, that guy was a real idiot. No one could do anything right according to him."

"But," I would ask, "what about the other three bosses you have had?"

"They weren't much better. Let me tell you about. . . ."

Just about anyone will follow someone whose authority seems legitimate. People with authority problems, however, do not readily grant such legitimacy. They do not easily give respect, and thus obedience, to others. Such people implicitly demand that authorities first prove themselves worthy.

Every one of us has, at one time or another, been "judged and found wanting by our inferiors." The best and most able people do not always end up with the most power. Almost daily we face the challenge of getting along with people who, despite the fact that they have power over us, may be less qualified than we are. The king, in other words, may be incompetent.

This proverb is exhorting us to open our eyes and reckon with what is before us. "Look," the writer seems to be saying, "the king (or the boss) can hurt you. Don't ignore his (her) threats by sticking your head in the sand and pretending that he (she) cannot. If you do not acknowledge the realities of power, you are your own worst enemy."

People who "ignore the king's threat" are often motivated by their own destructive psychodynamics. Something going on inside them is so driving that it impairs their ability to deal with reality. They are ever ready to do battle with "the big guy," the guy who carries the badge or signs the time cards. No one is going to talk to them like that!

When you scratch the surface of authority problems, you often discover that the person is really trying to work out a relationship with someone from the past, often a parent or sibling. The police officer or plant manager is simply an unconscious substitute. The rebellious person may actually be angry with Mom or Dad.

Probe one level deeper and you may well discover that underneath the anger is fear. The individual is afraid of the king! Beneath the rebellion are painful memories and a related fear of further punishment, psychological or physical.

If you find yourself in conflict with those in power, especially if this is a recurrent theme in your life, try to determine what (or whom) you may fear. And don't be afraid to consult a good therapist or counselor about it. Are you really fighting your father, your mother, your uncle, your aunt, your sister, or your brother? Don't dismiss these questions without addressing them honestly, because the answers may be subconscious for you.

Try to keep in mind that fear underlies almost all anger.

Questions for Reflection

To what extent do you ignore "the king's threat"?

Do you have the courage to admit that you are afraid when you are?

GUIDELINE 12: Never be one to give guarantees, or to pledge yourself as surety for another (22:26, REB).

The author of the proverb is saying, in essence, "Hold on to your power." Your money and your freedom are both forms of power. Do not relinquish them casually. Do not obligate yourself in self-destructive ways. Don't put everything on the line for someone else unless there's a very good reason to do so.

There is another message in this proverb. As hard as it may be, and as hard-hearted as it may sound, sometimes you just have to let others experience the consequences of their actions. You cannot always bail them out of trouble. If you try to, not only will you probably end up in trouble yourself, but they'll never learn to take care of themselves. Overprotectiveness only fosters dependence and immaturity.

Like just about every other clinical psychologist in the country, I have worked with many parents who had difficulty putting an end to their own overprotective behavior. One particular couple had raised an adopted son whose foremost expression of gratitude was repeatedly to get into trouble. Time after time they rescued him. Although they were not always conversant with the latest fad in child rearing (a definite plus), they really loved that kid. Finally, they stopped rescuing him. Within six months he straightened himself out. Sometimes if you want to help someone, you have to refuse to help.

Such advice can, of course, be used as an excuse for never helping anyone. The proverb is not intended to encourage people to abdicate their basic human responsibilities. Its author is simply trying to educate us about the lack of wisdom in always rushing in to fix things.

Perhaps because I was trained as a health care professional, I have often—far too often—tried to fix things for other people. It is sometimes easy for a psychologist to see what a person *ought* to do for his or her own good. Reflexively, I want the person to see it also—and then, to do it!

People, however, need time to grow and develop. They need to work out their own lives. There are reasons, sometimes deep and complicated ones, for why people end up in the situations they do. Efforts to save them can be frustrating and naive.

I once worked with a very gifted young doctor who, time and again, got himself into trouble with the power structure under which we both worked. This did not hurt his career much in the long run. He was very talented and, in certain ways, politically skillful, so he was able to land on his feet. He simply went to another job. But my behavior toward him hurt me!

On several occasions I tried earnestly to help him, and with hindsight I realize that he really didn't want help. Specifically, I tried to get him to modify his behavior so that he would stop alienating people. One night I stayed with him in his office until nearly ten o'clock—when I should have been home with my family—attempting to coach him. What a waste! What a mistake!

He was not open to coaching, and as I later found out he had no commitment to remaining in that organization anyway. But I did, because I believed that there was much good to be done and that both of us should stay there and do it. My own needs and wishes caused me not to see the obvious reality that, no matter what he said, he did not want to do anything but enhance his own career, without worrying much about whatever glass he might break along the way.

Be wise in choosing whom you try to rescue. Your time and energy are important. Once you spend them, they are gone forever and you cannot get them back in this life.

Ask yourself why others are foundering in the middle of the ocean without a life preserver. What did they do, or not do, to get thrown overboard? Do they want to be rescued? What exactly will it cost you?

Questions for Reflection

Whom, if anyone, are you currently trying to help?

Are you spending your time and energy wisely in these helping efforts?

Are there ways other than helping in which you are giving away your resources, and if so, are these good expenditures?

GUIDELINE 13: A simpleton believes every word; a clever person understands the need for proof (14:15, NEB).

Imagine your favorite evening news commentator announcing how a medical researcher has discovered that cancer patients have an unusually low level of a certain vitamin in their bodies. This researcher, we are told by the commentator, has repeated these measurements at several hospitals across the country and the results have been verified. *Time* is going to run the discovery as its cover story. What would happen?

People who have cancer, or who fear that they might, would probably run out to buy a lot of vitamin supplements.

Yet there would be a major problem with all of this. Even if cancer patients do show a specific vitamin deficiency, this does not prove that the deficiency caused the cancer. Both cancer and the vitamin deficiency could have been caused by some third thing yet to be discovered.

You could argue that, were there only a 1 percent chance that the vitamin prevents or cures cancer, it is well worth taking the supplements. This might be true—unless, of course, there was a medical reason not to take them. The point remains, however, that most people would be unable or unwilling to reason this all out. Let me offer two more brief examples:

Claim: Bigger cars are safer because there are fewer fatalities in luxury cars.

Analysis: Yes, but older people drive the luxury cars because, as a rule, only they can afford them. The little cars are more often driven by young people who, clearly, take more unnecessary risks. (Note: Large cars probably *are* safer, but the effect of who drives what size car has to be taken into consideration.)

Claim: More ice cream is sold in the summertime, which is also when more people drown. Obviously, eating ice cream causes people to drown.

Analysis: You've got to be kidding!

Most of us are gullible in one way or another. Some people are quick to believe hot tips. Others readily believe certain kinds of news stories. Still others are easily conned by salespersons. Education is supposed to build into us some healthy doubt, and to some extent it does. Well-educated people are usually less likely to believe something just because it is in print or because some famous person says it. Yet we all have psychological needs to believe certain kinds of things. What we need to believe may differ greatly from what the person next to us needs to believe.

If the orb in which you function is a sophisticated one, what you can afford to accept as "proof" becomes critical. In some business settings, for example, highly intelligent people routinely make false claims because, in one way or another, this helps their careers. These people are often charismatic, impressive, and believable, and sometimes slick and self-serving. You will accept what they say *only* at your peril.

Weigh carefully what others claim to be true. Although no one can function effectively from a paranoid position, it is important to exercise appropriate skepticism. Human motives can be exceedingly complex. Always ask yourself what the potential payoff might be to the person making a claim if you believed the claim and then acted on it. Even the best people can have bad motives now and then.

Questions for Reflection

In what specific areas, if any, do you tend to "believe" too quickly?

What sorts of claims are you most predisposed to accept?

Toward which individuals might you wisely exercise more discretionary caution?

Going All Out

GUIDELINE 14: Hard work always yields its profit, idle talk brings only want (14:23, NJB).
The lazy hunter puts up no game; those who are diligent reap a rich harvest (12:27, REB).

There are few shortcuts to success. Although some people work hard and never succeed, few of us ever succeed without working hard. Some highly successful people who have almost killed themselves to achieve what they have make it appear that they never strained harder than to sign autographs or endorse checks. There is sometimes great poise in this. Great art is to make it look easy.

The rock-hard truth, however, is that few actresses are "discovered" on the Malibu Beach; few corporation presidents coast their way to the top; and, few millionaires acquire their wealth by throwing darts at the business section of the newspaper.

One reason for shunning hard work is that it can be painful. Just about no one likes to put in fourteen-hour days—except workaholics who stay at the office so they don't have to go home. Unless work is your way of avoiding something, it takes a lot of discipline to stay at it after your eyes start burning and your back muscles begin to ache. It is so much more appealing to sit in front of the television or to crawl into bed. People who win Nobel Prizes forgo these pleasures. In psychological jargon, they "delay gratification." If you want to achieve, you have to be willing to put in effort and, sometimes, to endure considerable pain.

Moreover, you may have to do this over a long period of time. For work of any major significance to succeed, it usually has to be sustained. This is what the "tortoise and hare" fable is about. To read a long book, you have to keep at it, working your way through page after page, chapter after chapter. Large houses are built of many bricks.

Some of us refuse to work hard for reasons other than lack of fortitude or endurance. Some people consider hard work the backbone of our civilization; others regard it as the royal road to the coronary care unit. Some people lust for fame and fortune; others are content with being an ordinary person. Some people are willing to divide their loyalties between work and family, or even to sacrifice the latter for the former; others do not want to deprive themselves or their loved ones of even one minute they could otherwise spend together. A person who clearly understands the high price of success, refuses to pay it, and then accepts the consequences is probably in pretty good psychological shape. Such a person is wisely "counting the cost" before signing the contract. However, some of us shy away from hard work for reasons that are less healthy.

When I was in college, I would sometimes not study for an examination until the night before I had to take it. If I got an A, I was able to congratulate myself for being smart. If I ended up with a lesser grade, I could say to myself, "Why, of course. I didn't have enough time to study." By using these tactics, I was able to preserve my self-image as quite a clever fellow, no matter what. Although I wouldn't have admitted it at the time, I was probably afraid of failure.

As the author of the first proverb seems to suggest, some of us use talking as a substitute for acting. Words can serve a number of truly incredible psychological functions, among them the creation of comforting illusions. We can use words as mechanisms of magic. For example, by making endless lists of what we intend to do, we can avoid ever doing anything. By "talking a good game" in the business world, we can endlessly put off ever actually having to play.

It is important to review your words-to-work ratio from time to time, to make sure that you are not fooling yourself. Taking inventory once in a while can help you remain on the road that you most wish to travel.

Questions for Reflection

Are you clear about your professional goals, and about how these relate to your other goals?

Are you putting in enough effort to achieve what you want?

Are you backing away from all-out effort because you fear failure?

Are there areas in which you use words as a magical substitute for work?

GUIDELINE 15: Diligence brings people to power (12:24, REB).

The world is full of people who are in positions of major responsibility because they proved trustworthy. They did their homework as well as their best. They demonstrated that they could do one thing effectively, often through being willing to put in a little extra effort, and then were asked to do something more significant. In this way they ascended their particular career ladders, rung by rung.

A friend of mine began working years ago in a small Sun Belt bank. His starting position was modest, but he was soon promoted to a post of more importance. Within a couple of years, he was getting offers from other banks. Not long after that, he accepted a position in the San Francisco office of one of the largest financial institutions in the country. He continued to do well and was promoted, again and again.

Eventually, he "retired" from this institution. Taking the money he had accumulated, he set about multiplying it. This, too, he did with great success. I have never been brash enough to ask him to tell me his net worth, but I know it is substantial.

"How did you do it?" I asked. "You're still a young man."

"When I worked for the banks," he said, "I would always work a little harder than everyone else. I did a little extra and stayed just a little ahead. When one of the senior vice presidents would ask me to do something, I would quietly agree and promise to have it done within a week or two. Most of the time I had already done it and the report was in my desk drawer. I'd just wait a couple days and then deliver it. I was usually able to beat out even the Harvard MBAs. I've done the same thing with my investments. I just work hard."

I think it would be more accurate to say that he worked diligently. Diligence denotes not only hard work but also a certain attention to detail. It means working smarter. Careful and consistent effort is normally a prerequisite to getting promoted or capturing a larger share of a market, both of which constitute an increase in power.

Power is an elusive object of study. It is not tangible, like a poker chip or a banknote, but intangible, perhaps like a hypnotic trance. How much power an individual enjoys in any domain often changes constantly. One definition of power is that it is the capacity to influence others, make things happen, and get your own way. There is, of course, formal and informal power—how the organizational chart says things work versus how they really work. And a person's power can rise or fall dramatically on the strength of a single decision.

Some writers of books about business success regard power as an end in itself, which is shortsighted. Power is better thought of as a means. It enables you to get things done, whether good or bad. "Power corrupts, and absolute power corrupts absolutely." Perhaps. Although power can corrupt, it can also prove ennobling. If you are a decent person—and you probably wouldn't have opened this book if you weren't—you might as well wield as much power as you can. Otherwise, someone far less decent may do the job instead. Be careful, however. Power has turned countless otherwise good human beings into monsters.

Diligently serve those around you and you will almost certainly be entrusted with some kind of power. If you already have power, you will probably be given more.

Questions for Reflection

In what areas could you serve more diligently?

At this time in your career, how do you regard power?

How much power do you have?

How much do you want?

GUIDELINE 16: Schemes lightly made come to nothing, but with detailed planning they succeed (15:22, REB).

J. R. R. Tolkien worked on his *Lord of the Rings* trilogy for many years before he submitted it for publication. Tolkien was not in a hurry. An accomplished scholar, he knew how long it usually takes to turn out something first-rate. His close attention to plot, character, and, most of all, language yielded great rewards. Quite aside from whatever fame and fortune these books bestowed on their author or his estate, they represent a lasting contribution to literature.

Such painstaking effort runs counter to some of our most cherished values. The majority of people in our society are impressed more with speed than forethought. Yet it has been correctly observed that, most of the time, no one will remember how fast you did something, only how well—which means planning. Great business leaders are often known for their ability to plan ahead.

When I was in my twenties, an older friend and I met for breakfast every few weeks to discuss, among other things, possible business ventures. We considered hundreds of ideas, some of them promising. Whenever we stumbled onto something that I regarded as a "winner," I almost always wanted to get on with it immediately. He, by contrast, pressed for more reflection, more planning. Being a wise man with considerable business savvy and experience, he did this gently and always applauded me for creativity. Yet, in his wisdom, he understood that the difference between success and failure often hinges on careful forethought.

As a result of the time I spent with him, I eventually came up with a couple hundred business ideas and, to this day, pride myself on having launched only a few of them. But, the ones I did launch worked. They did not make me rich, but they did succeed in the marketplace, including *Clinician's Research Digest*, which I founded and sold to the American Psychological Association. That publication is still going strong.

Sometimes the shortest distance to a goal is *not* a beeline. The core issue here is real versus illusory efficiency. By rushing around, doing lots of irrelevant work, you can convince yourself that you are accomplishing something when, in fact, you are doing little more than tiring yourself out. We have only so much time, energy, and capital. Squandering these resources by spending them prematurely is like shooting off the fireworks a week before the celebration. When the right time comes, there may be nothing left.

Samurai warriors were notorious for their efficiency. Economy of effort was the hallmark of their skill. Every shift of the body, every movement of the sword, was purposeful. Nothing wasted, nothing random. What Westerners tend to miss about the samurai is that their minds were trained for battle every bit as much as their bodies were. They were trained to think in a way that made their actions almost afterthoughts.

Most highly effective business people are like samurai. Their major battlefields lie in the territories of their minds. What they actually do is merely the concrete expression of their invisible mental battle. Unfortunately, most of us join the battle on the wrong field, whether it is the boardroom, the golf course, or the negotiation table.

If you want to do your best, you have to sit down with that ugly yellow pad—I prefer white myself—and start scribbling. Make lists, draw boxes, draft flowcharts, construct graphs. Sometimes the most beneficial action you can take is simply to sit there, with the pad on your lap, and do nothing but think. I have been amazed at how reluctant people are to do this, lest they waste precious time. Like certain species of animals separated from food by a glass barrier, they hopelessly try to push through instead of walk around it.

I believe it was management guru Peter Drucker who first said that one hour of planning is worth at least ten hours of work. What, then, are the tangible benefits of planning?

First, you can see problems coming and work out solutions in advance. Tackle little problems before they grow into big ones. It is easier to uproot baby weeds than to rid a garden of fully developed underbrush.

Second, you can better evaluate the true merits and demerits of your various alternatives. It is easier to do cost-benefit or risk-benefit assessments when you are not under pressure.

Third, you make yourself more likely to consult others who can help you gain perspective. One translation (NRSV) of this proverb is "Without counsel, plans go wrong, but with many advisers they succeed."

Fourth, and most important of all, you will be less likely to avoid doing productive work by immersing yourself into frenetic and misguided activity. Don't be one of those people who are working so hard that they can't make any money. This, of course, is a metaphor as well as, for some individuals, a reality. As a metaphor, I take it to mean this: Do the high-leverage things.

If you want to move a heavy boulder, you will accomplish little by pushing harder. Before you become exhausted, think about what might actually help you move it. As the cliché has it, plan your work and work your plan.

As much as you can, run your work life as the samurai fought their battles, in the mind—make *this* your private command center.

Questions for Reflection

How much do you run away from uncertainty, and the tension it brings, by misguided flights into action?

Is there anything about which you need to plan more thoroughly before taking further action?

GUIDELINE 17: Wealth hastily gotten will dwindle, but those who gather little by little will increase it (13:11, NRSV).

Whether a particular person moves in the direction of accumulating wealth seems to depend a great deal on his or her economic habits. Does the person save or spend? Take intelligent risks or play irrational long shots?

Such economic habits are often greatly affected by how quickly one acquires financial resources. Have they come all at once, perhaps the result of winning the lottery? Or have they come through years of consistent and painstaking effort? One's experiences condition one's attitudes, which in turn set the stage for one's future behavior. The proverb writer is contrasting the likely attitudes of the person who, step by step, accumulates resources versus those of the person who has perhaps enjoyed a windfall profit.

To do almost anything well requires discipline. People who suddenly come into money typically underestimate the amount of work that goes into the proper care of wealth. This is why the news often carries stories of persons who have tragically squandered inheritances or who, having made a financial killing, immediately turn around and lose their entire fortunes.

Those who hold on to their gains and continue to increase them have usually learned to save, to sacrifice, and to scrutinize carefully their own financial actions. Through years of practice, most have developed good economic attitudes and habits. Successful accumulators seem to share a number of characteristics.

First, they tend to view the accumulation of resources as a way of life, not a blitzkrieg. People who attempt to lose weight through fad diets usually fail. If they do lose a few pounds, they are almost certain to gain them back within a short time. By contrast, people who change their basic habits and attitudes often accomplish their weight-control goals. They learn to eat more slowly, to monitor conscientiously their caloric intakes, to resist making social occasions out of meals, to develop substitute behaviors for running to the refrigerator, and so on.

Similarly, people who amass wealth learn to indulge less frequently, to spend less lavishly, to resist the acquisition of trendy gimmicks and questionable gadgets, to refuse the use of credit for consumption (but not necessarily for convenience or investment leverage), and to abstain from jumping on the bandwagon of frivolous crazes. Perhaps most important of all, successful accumulators tend to keep and periodically review records of everything they spend. This can be an enlightening and painful process. It is hard to confront one's economic sins!

Second, effective accumulators tend to reinvest the yields from previously successful investments. They do not "take profits" to go on spending sprees. Some investment counselors speak of this as "not eating one's monetary children." Good investors have the progressive mentality of that legendary mathematician who, when asked by the caliph what he wanted as payment for counting the ruler's armies, replied, "One grain of wheat for the first square on the chessboard, two grains for the second square, four for the third, eight for the fourth . . ."

Third, despite their relentless movement in the direction of accumulation, the economically successful are characteristically not stingy or cheap. They know, for example, that it is not worth the loss of others' respect and goodwill to get hung up on whether a dinner check has been divided precisely. Their images are worth far more than a few dollars. And they do not wait for a good investment to come down a few cents before they buy or, alternatively, for their profits to go up a few cents before they sell.

There is another dimension to this proverb that is worth noting. Some translations of "wealth hastily gotten" imply "that which one has acquired dishonorably." If one is unlikely to acquire good economic habits through windfall profits, how much prudence can one expect to learn through theft? Con men do not make good investment fund managers, even when they are managing their own funds.

If you want the blessings of wealth, proceed with determination, discipline, and honor.

Questions for Reflection

Are you financially persistent?

Do you exercise sufficient economic discipline?

Do you track what you spend?

Do you think in terms of the future value of each dollar (a dollar wisely invested today will be worth many dollars tomorrow)?

Wisdom of the Tongue

GUIDELINE 18: The lips of the righteous know what is fitting, but the mouth of the wicked only what is perverse (10:32, NIV).

Goodness, or what the Bible terms "righteousness," is closely related to graciousness. Good-hearted people are gracious people. They are positive, considerate, loving.

Some people, however, always seem to see the negative. They are critical and inflexible. Unlike people who extend themselves to say things that are appropriate and constructive, they carp, grouse, and complain without regard for what this does to others. There will always be those who opportunistically use just about any occasion that comes along to express their anger and bitterness, often at someone else's expense.

The author of the proverb seems to be saying that good people care enough about others to say the right things, while bad people care only about discharging their venomous spleens. The latter are rigidly locked into "perverse" talk. Another translation (REB) renders this as "subversive talk." The proverb writer is contrasting the person who knows and says what is fitting with the person who chronically foments malice.

How does one always say the socially fitting thing without becoming a Pollyanna or a hypocrite? What if someone or something is truly terrible, even evil?

Suppose the boss ruthlessly, and without cause, fires someone who has five young children to support.

Suppose everyone around you is viciously picking on the new kid, just for the sport of it.

94

Suppose the person on whom you rely most directly openly sabotages you.

This proverb is not advocating passivity. There are times when the worst thing you could possibly do would be to keep your mouth shut.

"Mr. Martin, I would like to ask you if you could possibly consider reinstating Jim Hill. I'd be glad to work with him to make sure that he does his job exactly the way you want. Maybe I could give him a little time each night after we close."

"Come on, you guys have had your fun. Leave the kid alone. Give him a few months to get to know us before you roast him."

"John, come in here. I need to speak with you privately. You've worked for me for a long time now. Is it true that you . . . ?"

These are good things to say. They are tactful, yet strong. Such statements can also involve risk. Mr. Martin may tell you to follow Jim Hill out the door. The mob may turn on you as well as the new kid. Your subordinate may sabotage you all the more violently in the future for daring to bring up the matter. Nonetheless, the best thing to do in each case is probably to speak up when the time seems right.

At issue is whether we can respond to what is in front of us—to reality. Can we speak and act in a way that "fits" what is going on, or are we one-note negativists, stuck in the groove of character assassination? Can we rise above such negativity, or are we doomed to inject it into everything, to make it part of our life-script?

The person who penned this proverb seems to be telling us that one route to more effective social behavior is goodness. If your heart is pure, your actions will be "fitting." Since others reward us, in business and elsewhere, for appropriate social conduct, goodness has its practical advantages. However much negative talk may please others at the moment, no one likes or trusts a rigidly critical person. This is because people sense, usually correctly, that they could quickly become targets of criticism.

To function at your best, inspire in others the confidence that you can be trusted *not* to turn them into targets. Keep your heart pure and your speech gracious.

Questions for Reflection

How appropriate have your words been during the past several days?

How given are you to subversive talk?

What, if anything, triggers unproductive negativity in you?

How might you avoid getting caught up in destructive discussions?

GUIDELINE 19: Don't talk so much. You keep putting your foot in your mouth. Be sensible and turn off the flow (10:19, TLB).

Deep in the brain is a set of neural structures that together are known as the limbic system. This system of interacting brain structures is the primary seat of emotionality. When certain parts of the limbic system are overstimulated, we develop very strong feelings, ranging from rage to terror.

One way to overactivate your limbic system is to talk too much, which is perhaps why we use the expression "to keep one's peace" in connection with being quiet. Once these emotional centers are overactivated, we tend to talk all the more. In this fashion, a vicious circle can be set off by launching into a conversation too quickly. While there is nothing wrong with emotions per se, and certainly nothing wrong with talking, overly intense emotional states can prompt us to say imprudent things. What we say, as a result, can become convoluted, complex.

As a psychotherapist, I learned to be wary of too much complexity in human affairs. When things become overly complicated, something unwholesome is usually going on. People do *not* do their best when they are trying to run in different directions at the same time, or when they are simply moving about randomly, without a clear purpose. Because we are, by nature, both thinking and feeling beings, it is important that we balance the cognitive and emotional sides of ourselves. We need to experience our feelings without acting on every one of them. Talking too much makes us more vulnerable to emotional and behavioral chaos. This is the key message behind the recent work on "emotional intelligence."

The crucial thing to avoid is making public statements in an attempt to work out private problems. People who talk too much are almost always trying to reduce their inner tensions, to resolve mental conflicts. Reducing tensions and resolving conflicts are desirable, but the price for doing this via committee meetings or sales conferences is too high. It would be better to talk to yourself in the mirror.

Another translation of this proverb (REB) renders it as "When there is too much talk, offence is never far away; the prudent hold their tongues." Note that, while other proverbs deal with the undesirability of gossip, this one concerns the relationship between talk and action within an individual. Somehow, excessive talk makes us more likely to "sin." An ancient way of understanding sin is "missing the mark." The distance between the bull's-eye of an archer's target and his arrow was called "sin." We are more likely to miss the mark when we compulsively talk.

Psychologists who specialize in the study of learning speak of "response latency." By this they mean the time it takes a person to react to something. When we talk too much, we typically have short latencies. Instead of counting to three before we speak, we rush in—where even angels might "fear to tread"!

If you tend at times to say more than you should, there are a few things you can do that may help.

First, do not let yourself talk until you feel that you have the necessary composure. Try to interrupt the limbic-tongue "reflex." Regard the buildup of tension as a sign that you probably should *wait*, especially if you are prone to use public conversation to reduce this tension.

Second, work on increasing your response latencies. Begin by keeping track of how long it usually takes you to respond to what someone else says. One second? Two seconds? Three? Try to add a second a week to your latencies, until you get them where you believe they should be.

Third, use short sentences and paragraphs. Measure your words. Concentrate on saying what you have to say with style.

Fourth, if you need to lower your emotional reactivity in meetings, you might try taking along with you something to drain off your tension, for example, some paperwork. Make sure that you do this only if you can do it unobtrusively, without offending others.

Questions for Reflection

In which specific situations, if any, do you tend to talk too much?

If you do talk more than you would like, what concrete things could you do to inhibit your impulses to speak?

GUIDELINE 20: Be in no hurry to tell everyone what you have seen, or it will end in bitter reproaches from your friend (25:8, NEB).

During the first few years of my career, I felt a responsibility to tell the client everything that I discovered, as soon as I discovered it. Like many young therapists, I had to learn that good clinicians bide their time, waiting for the moment when the client is ready to hear. The therapist can have all kinds of insights, but these will prove of very limited value until the client is capable of absorbing them.

Most of us have considerable trouble accepting certain truths about ourselves. Who wants to be told unflattering things? We can find such information incredibly painful. Too much truth at one time overwhelms us and raises our defenses. It makes us feel threatened and helpless and, thus, usually angry.

In my personal as well as my professional life, I have struggled a great deal with the issue of self-disclosure. Many people, particularly in competitive environments, reveal almost nothing about themselves, lest it be used against them. They hide, rationalize, dissemble, and do almost anything they can to make you think only the best of them. This has always seemed spineless to me. And perhaps in reaction to such close-to-the-vest conduct, I decided long ago that withholding any information was always dishonest. I see now that this is not necessarily so.

People have just so much tolerance for confrontation. If we go around saying everything we think or feel, we will earn "bitter reproaches" even from our friends.

I suppose this proverb is also warning us against carrying tales. Few people like the bearer of bad tidings, which is why we hear talk, from time to time, about "slain messengers." A manager, despite temporary shows of interest, may not really *want* to know about the misdeeds of his or her employees. A husband or wife, similarly, may not want to know about the misconduct of a spouse. A parent may not want to hear that his or her child has misbehaved. Information can have powerful effects that are not always desirable. Naturally, there are times when it is right to deliver information, quite aside from whether the other person wants to hear it, but it takes good judgment to recognize when such times are upon us.

Not to say something when we feel the urge is to have to carry it around inside. It is sometimes difficult to do this, to "live in one's own head." I would much rather tell others what I think and feel, especially when it is about them, than reflect quietly by myself. I want to communicate. Contrary to a lot of mental health mythology, however, communication is not always desirable. Sometimes all it does is inflict pain.

Truly wise people know what to say and when to say it. Like accomplished athletes, they know the value of good timing. The right thing said at the wrong time can result in absolute disaster. Because they choose their words carefully, what they say is usually beneficial to others. It is also beneficial to them, since they do not sacrifice their relationships on the altars of verbal foolishness.

Watch. Listen. Reflect. As much as you can, become a keen observer. Attend especially to the sequences in which people say things. Draw your conclusions, and, if they are negative, weigh carefully whether stating them is likely to do any good.

What might it cost you to say what you are thinking? When you are forced to pit your integrity against your safety, the decision can only be made by you. In the contemporary business world—and perhaps it has always been so—safety tends to prevail over integrity. This, of course, is not a good thing.

Questions for Reflection

When and to which people are you likely to say too much?

When you are about to say something that another person will find painful, do you focus more on his or her welfare or on your own need to talk?

GUIDELINE 21: Do not speak in the hearing of a fool, who will only despise the wisdom of your words (23:9, NRSV).

To talk with someone is to make an investment. Each of us has only a finite amount of time on earth, and we can spend some of it conversing personally with only a small number of people. When you talk with someone, you are spending part of your life. Let me make this a bit more concrete.

In the typical human life, there are somewhere between twenty-five thousand and thirty-five thousand days. In the ordinary work year, there are between 2,000 and 2,500 hours. A week consists of 168 hours, of which we sleep 50 to 60, leaving roughly 110 hours for everything else. As opposed to what we thought when we were very young, a lifetime does not last forever. Ultimately, there is no such thing as "free time." Any time we use we pay for dearly, since it never comes again.

This proverb advises us to spend our time and energy wisely, to make good interpersonal investments. Contrary to a lot of ridiculous rhetoric, everyone is not equally worthy of one's time. The writer seems to be saying, "Don't waste your life energy." Investing it in someone who lacks either the capacity or the will to learn is to waste some of your substance.

As I write this, I think of all the people in my life who have become angry with me because I did not give them as much of my time as they wanted. Perhaps I should feel flattered, and I vaguely remember that, early in my childhood, I wanted to be sought after in this manner. Now, as a man well into middle age, I just resent the insensitivity of people who think nothing of becoming time thieves.

It's *my* life, a sacred trust account, to manage according to my best judgment. It is my job to be the wisest trustee of this account that I can, not to surrender its management, blindly and irresponsibly, to others. No matter what, we should spend our lives in the way that *we* think we should, even if this offends the whole world!

But the author of the proverb is also getting at something else. He is advising us to "watch what we say around foolish people." Saying the wrong thing to someone who might mindlessly repeat it is surely to ask for trouble. And saying even the right thing to someone who does not have the good sense to appreciate it is only to court pain.

Sometimes, our own good-heartedness outweighs our good sense. At least, this is the case with me. While I have always been extremely careful about protecting the confidences of others, I have not always been so careful to protect my own. Thus, I have occasionally shared information about myself that later I was sorry I had. My intent was to help the other person, but my reward was to suffer. For the sake of perspective, I should add that, on sum, personal sharing has been more of a benefit than a cost, but the point of the proverb remains: use good judgment in what you say to whom. As Francis Bacon suggested, "Knowledge is power." To give others knowledge about you is often to give them power over you.

Another translation (REB) renders the first part of this proverb "Do not address yourself to a stupid person." Perhaps the love of wisdom is a kind of intelligence all its own, while the distaste for wisdom, even in a technical genius, is a singular kind of stupidity. If so, the challenge of this proverb is to be able to distinguish among the different types of intelligence. The whiz kid down the hall who earned his MBA from Stanford at twenty-one and who can do regression equations in his sleep may not have much of an aptitude for wisdom!

Protect yourself. Spend your time and energy wisely. "Do not throw your pearls before swine."

Here are some hints that may help prevent you from saying more than you should:

- "Let me think that one through before I offer an opinion."
- "I'd prefer not to comment—if I did, I wouldn't feel right."
- "That's an interesting question . . . [purposeful silence]."

Questions for Reflection

Are you spending your time and energy wisely or wasting them in unfruitful conversations?

Are you sharing confidences with the right people?

Are there particular people who seem to draw you into saying more than you should and, if so, how might you stop this?

GUIDELINE 22: Even a fool, if he holds his peace, is thought wise; keep your mouth shut and show your good sense (17:28, NEB).

Shortly after I entered college, I attended a party in Manhattan. It was hosted by my prep school senior English teacher, who had invited several of his old friends: psychoanalysts, artists, and so on. One of his guests was a clean-cut man of about fifty who, as I recall, had won a prestigious architectural prize when he was a student at Yale. He was intelligent, urbane, and wise. It did not take long for us to become immersed in conversation, because I very much wanted to learn everything I could from him.

I clearly remember him saying this: "If you enter a room full of strangers and simply keep your mouth shut, people will imagine all sorts of wonderful things about you. But once you start talking, you begin to dissuade them of their illusions." A related Confucian proverb states, "Better to be thought a fool than to open one's mouth and confirm it."

Lying low or "cutting a low profile," as it is called, is sometimes a magnificently effective way to enhance your prestige. Perhaps other people need to talk so much that they are grateful to you for giving them a chance, and so they reward you by thinking well of you. Perhaps just about everyone wants to have heroes and heroines, so that all you have to do is provide them with a blank screen and they will "project" onto you the heroic qualities that they hold most dear. Whatever the psychological mechanisms underlying the benefits of lying low, these benefits can be considerable. For one thing, being quiet gives you the chance to listen. And, as suggested above, you enhance your image of sagacity and thus your persuasive influence.

I want to add some qualifications to these statements that derive from social psychology. First, you cannot expect endless silence to make you look like Einstein. At least once in a while you have to say something intelligent. However, a porpoise could probably meet this requirement, by choosing wisely from among the possible things it might think of to say. Again, if you speak sparingly and thus treat what others say with attentive respect, they will naturally evaluate whatever you do choose to say in a favorable light. The whole thing is a little bit like money and inflation. When there's too much money or chatter, value declines.

Second, some research suggests that people who talk more, as opposed to less, are generally assumed by others to be more competent. From carefully watching others in high-level meetings over the years, I have come to the conclusion that the key issue is not quantity of speech but dominance. People who talk more tend to be more dominant, and it is their dominance (i.e., their assertiveness) that prompts others to evaluate them as competent. They give the impression of knowing what to do. It is no secret that people who talk too much—those who overcommunicate—quickly become known as blowhards, not to be trusted with bundling last week's newspapers.

There is probably a trade-off between dominance and quiet, namely, others will tend to see you as more dominant if you talk more rather than less—unless, of course, others put you down in public and get away with it. Combining an assertive with a measured approach probably works best. The ultimate ideal is probably quiet strength, that is, positioning yourself so that, on those rare occasions when you speak, others listen. If you are too dominant, they will resent you; although they may perceive you as more competent, they may no longer entertain all those wonderful fantasies about you that silence can foster, and this may prove a significant loss. What you say and how you say it both count. Others "take off" for mistakes in either domain and thus deduct points for both bad style and shallow content.

The proverb we are considering is really saying something like this: if you do not know what you're talking about, keep quiet and let others enjoy their wonderful fantasies about you, fantasies that will only be augmented if you are sincerely interested in what they have to say. If, however, you know what you're talking about and others are ready to listen, perhaps you should take the risk of saying what you think.

Questions for Reflection

Do you maintain your silent poise, or do you tend to destroy the good things others might think about you by talking too readily?

In what specific situations, and with which specific people, do you tend most to lose your poise?

When Modesty Helps

GUIDELINE 23: Better to be a nobody and yet have a servant than pretend to be somebody and have no food (12:9, NIV).

All of us know people who are obnoxious in their arrogance. They communicate that they should be served, that others are beneath them, that they are too good to do what they expect the rest of us to be willing to do, for example, to take minutes, write on flip charts, make calls, or empty wastebaskets. Such persons are not usually popular. Others see them as offensively proud and pretentious.

Most human endeavors turn on the axis of social relationships. A common misconception about business, for example, is that what matters most is the bottom line. The truth is that the bottom line is rarely the bottom line. While a for-profit enterprise has to be profitable to survive, and the CEO and other senior officers will always focus their attentions keenly on the bottom line, even they will inevitably be concerned with all sorts of things that have little or nothing directly to do with money. People will often tell you that they are working for a larger home, a bigger share of the company, a greater share of the pie, or a luxurious yacht. Although such claims may be true, such goals rarely account for how hard they work.

We all want to value ourselves, to enjoy the esteem of ourselves and others—the latter is known as "status." When you act in an arrogant manner, you put others down and, in the process, detract from their esteem. When others see us as bragging, we may be intending only to express our confidence, to share our joy, and to delight in our own achievements and capacities, quite aside from how these compare with anyone else's. Yet such behavior can raise others' anxieties, depress them, and lead them to feel worthless and inadequate.

Out of my own natural enthusiasm, I tend at times to act expansively. Occasionally, I notice that, instead of joining in my celebrations, others pull back and sometimes look overtly despondent. I have had to remind myself, over the years, to consider the effects of my self-congratulations on them and to admit that others may experience my innocent boasts as a subtle form of hostile dominance. To them, the message that comes through, intended or not, is "I am better than you."

This proverb is warning us that there can be serious consequences to pretense, perhaps even when we do not intend to be pretentious. We can lose our jobs or, perhaps worse in the long run, our friends. Arrogance and pretentiousness may not be exactly the same, but they often go hand in hand.

Another translation (NEB) of this proverb is "It is better to be modest and earn one's living than to be conceited and go hungry." We could just as well substitute the word *inflated* for *conceited*. Thus the proverb would read "It is better to be modest and earn one's living than to be inflated and go hungry." Our inflations are usually others' deflations. Psychological research has amply supported the idea that a little modesty does, indeed, make us more attractive to others.

Naturally, there are qualifications. Too much modesty makes you look incompetent, like an obsequious buffoon. A blunder by a public figure, say a politician or a scientist, will make an audience like him or her more, but only if they regard this figure as possessing considerable status. For the president of the company to spill coffee on himself may help him or her seem more human, more approachable. For the janitor to spill coffee may only make him or her seem clumsy. Pratfalls, as they are called, seem to enhance your standing with others only if you have a substantial edge already. Modesty is like that also. It has to be seen by others to fall within the right range if it is to help you.

If you tend to be more expansive about your own achievements and abilities than you should be, adjust your self-presentation so that you are less likely to offend others. But don't go too far in the opposite direction!

Questions for Reflection

How modest do you tend to be—how do others perceive you?

Are there situations in which you tend to be too expansive or too reserved?

Are there people whose feelings you may be hurting just by telling them how well things are going for you?

Are you injuring your reputation or your chances for advancement by too loudly blowing your own horn?

GUIDELINE 24: A fool thinks that he is always right (12:15, NEB).
A clever person conceals his knowledge, but a stupid one blurts out folly (12:23, REB).

"My mind is made up—don't confuse me with the facts!"

This is the attitude that the first of these two proverbs seems to be warning against. All of us have had the experience of trying to get others to listen when they just did not want to hear. They "knew what was what," and there was little chance of getting them to change their opinions.

Sometimes the people who are the least well informed speak the loudest and with the most conviction. They buttress their beliefs and illusions with sheer passion and mindless bluster. "I must be right. Can't you hear how loud I'm speaking?"

I have seen at least one person's career ruined because he so strongly maintained, and loudly broadcast, opinions that were plainly silly to everyone else. It seemed that the more foolish the opinion, the more vehemently he held it. Eventually, he developed a reputation for incompetence. At that point, even if he had won the Pulitzer Prize, it would not have helped. I felt sorry for him. He was his own worst enemy.

Why do we sometimes close our minds? What is it that impels us sometimes to talk the most when we know the least?

Psychologists who study perception—how we see, hear, and so on—refer to the principle of closure. By this, they mean that we all have a powerful natural tendency to finish whatever is incomplete. If, for example, we see a circle or a square with a piece missing, we have an almost irresistible urge to fill in the missing piece. Even if we do not take out a pencil, we complete the figure in our minds. We want things to be complete, neatly tied up, no loose strings hanging about and, most of all, no missing parts.

Intelligence is in part the ability to resist premature closure, that is, it is the capacity to wait until one has sufficiently analyzed a problem before drawing conclusions. A great deal of research has demonstrated that people who get fixated do not make good problem solvers. Their thinking is too rigid, too conventional. And intellectual rigidity generally increases with anxiety. The more threatened we feel, the less flexible our thinking usually becomes and the more we tend to close our minds. To think well, we have to stay loose.

Anxiety also seems to lie at the root of our tendency to "broadcast our folly." Harvard philosopher George Santayana once said that a fanatic is someone who, having lost sight of his purpose, redoubles his efforts. We are all a little like that. When we begin to wonder if we really know something, especially when this something is important to us, we often try all the harder to convince ourselves that we do. One way we do this is to hold forth more intensely.

Instead of facing our uncertainties, we attempt to obliterate them through a magical will to believe.

Another line of research suggests that we tend to justify our past actions. We do not like to be inconsistent. We like our behaviors and beliefs to line up nicely. Hence, we will argue vehemently for principles that are in accord with what we have already done, even if it is obvious to everyone else that what we did was a mistake. We are most in danger of "broadcasting our folly" when we have already done something foolish!

Now, about the wisdom of concealing our knowledge: The proverb is not telling us to hoard knowledge, refusing to give it to others when they can profit from it; it is telling us to err on the side of understatement rather than over-statement. The writer is advising us to exercise prudent judgment about what we say, instead of spilling our intellectual guts at every turn.

The second proverb could be taken to mean "People who talk a lot cannot possibly know what they are talking about, since those who truly know do not talk!" This resembles the more modern proverb "Still waters run deep."

Questions for Reflection

How much do you tend to compound your errors by publicly justifying your mistakes?

Are there particular topics on which you tend quickly to close your mind?

In which situations, if any, do you too readily broadcast your knowledge?

Are you generally able to determine when and when not to speak (see Ecclesiastes 3)?

GUIDELINE 25: Poverty and disgrace come to him who ignores instruction, but he who heeds reproof is honored (13:18, RSV).
The way to honour is humility (15:33b, NEB).

Few of us like to be brought up short. There is just something that makes us bristle under criticism. Our tendency is to fight back, to discount what is being said, to justify ourselves. Often, as a defense, we impugn the motives or the competence of the person criticizing us. Yet, as another translation (REB) of the first proverb warns, "To refuse correction brings poverty and humilia-tion." Our resistance to learning from others' criticisms, regardless of whether these "others" are friends or foes, can hurt our financial well-being as well as our social standing.

Most psychologists can usually predict, during the initial interview, how much a new client is likely to profit from their assistance. Intelligence is, of course, a plus. Clients who are bright are more able to grasp life's subtleties. Anxiety usually helps too. Clients who are in acute misery are usually more motivated to work. And optimism helps. Clients who expect things to get better and to accomplish something typically have the endurance to stick with the process when it becomes painful. What seems to help most of all, however, is the simple willingness to learn. The people who best learn life's lessons are those who possess the humility to accept its teachings.

I have had the good fortune to get to know many top executives in widely diverse industries. What amazes me about many of them is how open they are to feedback and criticism. They are by no means weak or indecisive; nor are they gluttons for punishment. As a group, senior executives tend to be strong, decisive, and tough. But they are also willing to examine themselves. To them, criticism is constructive, if only for the reason that it prompts them to think about something they might have ignored. It does not matter to them whether the person delivering the criticism is brilliant or ordinary, learned or amateurish, as long as what the person says seems credible. What does matter is the opportunity carried on the wings of any critique. Like successful people in any endeavor, they know how to turn potential liabilities into actual assets.

Many top-flight executives actively seek feedback from those under them, and many consulting companies, including my own, have developed highly specialized ways to provide it ("360s" and upward evaluation measures—see *www.relationaldynamics.com*).

"How am I doing?"

"Is there anything you think I ought to know about my performance?"

"Do you have any advice you could offer me?"

Doing this takes more courage than many people can muster. But the best leaders thrive on it, and the more they open themselves up to it, the stronger they become.

Naturally, you have to use good judgment in what you ask of whom. Certain people do not seem to have the good sense to appreciate openness and will, therefore, only hurt you if you ask them their opinion. Most of us, however, tend to miss out on a great deal of personal and professional growth simply because we are afraid to hear honest evaluations of our own behavior. Moreover, the more you open yourself to feedback, the less it can wound you. As a general rule, the more we face the things we fear, the less we fear them. By contrast, the fiery dragons of criticism become all the more ferocious when we run from them.

People who have the humility to listen, even when listening proves painful, tend to impress others as mature. They "come to honor" not only because they learn how to function better but also because others esteem them for their wisdom and stability.

When people take you to task, ask yourself if there is anything in what they say from which you might profit. Try to do this when they are firing their salvos or taking their best shots. At the very least, you can use the occasion as an opportunity to practice poise. If you are too reactive to criticism, say this to yourself: "I am not going to get sucked into defending my actions. What I am going to do is use this moment to practice listening." Admittedly, all this is hard to do, but it is usually well worth the effort.

Questions for Reflection

How do you generally respond to criticism?

To what extent do you view criticism as inherently valuable?

Is there a way to respond to feedback more constructively?

Whose feedback might you wisely seek out?

GUIDELINE 26: Pride goes before destruction and haughtiness before a fall (16:18, NLT).

History books are full of stories of how pride, of one kind or another, led to the downfall of a ruler. Hitler sent thousands of young men to their deaths simply because his pride would not allow him to see what would have been clear to any schoolchild: Germany had lost the war and the Thousand-Year Reich was over. Perhaps, to a man who had already massacred millions of innocent people, a few thousand more didn't much matter.

Business, too, has its share of stories to illustrate that "pride goeth before a fall." I suspect that the case studies cited in the early parts of this book are, in part, testimonies to misplaced pride. Such stories are not new. I well remember how much coverage the news media gave to the criminal indictment of an ex–General Motors wonder boy who, in the 1980s, launched his own automotive company. While this man worked for GM, he had become exceedingly critical of the giant corporation. Apparently, his independent business endeavor was as much a sincere protest as it was an entrepreneurial venture.

No doubt in part because of the depth of an economic recession, the car did not sell well, which placed its originator under considerable financial and psychological pressure. His response to poor sales was, according to his incredulous associates and employees, to increase production and, possibly, to become implicated in a multimillion-dollar cocaine sale. It seems as if the man's understandable pride in the car he had created made it impossible for him simply to admit defeat; ultimately, it seems to have led to his downfall.

Pride is the one stance or position, above all others, that can be our undoing. It is pride that prompts us to defend ourselves and not to listen. It is pride that impels us to attack those who dare to imply that we are anything less than perfect. It is our pride that is injured, most of the time, when our feelings are hurt.

"You only go around once, you know. Go for all the gusto you can. Don't wait for providence to make things fair in the end. Even the score now. Take what you know you should have." Sound familiar? This is roughly what the serpent is reputed to have told Eve in the garden of Eden.

We all seem to carry around inside ourselves our own invisible serpent that gets us right where it hurts, in the heart—in our pride. As a result, we sometimes stub our professional toes and fall on our personal faces.

Humankind's battle with pride goes back a long way. The ancient Greeks had a special word for pride, *hubris*. In the Greek tragedies, the protagonist was almost godlike. He had everything one could want. Unfortunately, he also routinely had this terrible, self-destructive pride. The Greek dramatists accurately perceived the lethality of pride and attempted to teach their contemporaries about its dangers. Their plays turn on the message "Don't be like them, these men who lost everything through hubris."

Be careful of defensive inflexibility, especially when it is combined with self-justification. Do not let pride ruin you. You deserve more than that.

Questions for Reflection

Is there an area of your life in which you are in trouble because of pride?

Is there something you should simply own up to and let it go at that?

Can you allow yourself to admit that you are less than perfect, especially with respect to those things in which you take pride?

GUIDELINE 27: Arrogance can inflame a city, but wisdom averts . . . anger (29:8, REB).
Fools are too arrogant to make amends; the upright know what reconciliation requires (14:9, REB).

The first of these two proverbs concerns arrogance by a person in authority, for example, by a boss. The second proverb has to do with ordinary relationships between people.

Arrogance in a ruler can be extremely provocative to those who are ruled. It can "inflame a whole city." Naturally, if the people who are ruled dare not speak out, the ruler may not know of their irritation and rage. It may stay hidden, underground, ready to surface at the first opportunity. This opportunity may be when the ruler is vulnerable, perhaps when the efficiency experts pass through or the management consultants come to do their climate surveys or leadership impact assessments. If those who are governed see the ruler as arrogant enough, there may be open rebellion in any event, no matter what the cost to those who rebel.

Managers who keep themselves arrogantly aloof from their subordinates are taking a big chance, especially if these subordinates feel they are being shunned because "they are not good enough, noble enough, smart enough, powerful enough, well-bred enough, educated enough," and so on. Holding yourself above others can be your downfall.

If you are the boss, then by definition you are above others in the organizational chart. They are, after all, your subordinates. But being in a certain position and therefore having to wield power is not the same thing as communicating to others that you are superior to them as people.

A once-popular book on how to succeed in the corporate corridors suggested that a truly powerful executive never goes to the photocopying machine, even if he or she repaired it six months earlier. Photocopying is simply beneath the dignity of a star. It conveys weakness and the likelihood of a limited future career.

There may be something to this. As sad as it may be, and as tragic a commentary on human nature as it may seem, doing "low-status" tasks may hurt one's public image and perhaps even injure one's chances for advancement. By contrast, the leaders who have been most respected throughout history seem to be those who were not afraid to get their hands dirty with work or to fight alongside, if not in front of, their troops.

I recommend that you *never* ask others to do what you yourself would not do. If you can photocopy, do it once in a while. If you can dial a phone, do that occasionally too, rather than bellowing to your assistant, "Get so-and-so on the phone." Obviously, sometimes we have people working so that they can do many of these routine tasks—tasks where they, not we, have what economists call "comparative advantage." I am not suggesting that the president of a large company begin wasting time—which is exactly what it would be—doing routine chores. I am suggesting, however, that if you are the boss, you communicate to your subordinates something along the lines of "We're all in this together. You have your job, and I have mine, but we are both people. Nothing you do is, in principle, beneath me. Nothing I do is, in principle, above you."

Now, about arrogance as an obstacle to reconciliation: Many people, in their efforts to shore up ailing self-images, adamantly refuse ever to say, "I'm sorry." They can neither forgive nor ask for forgiveness. Behind such people, almost always, are long trails of broken relationships. Most of these relationships could have been mended, healed, with just a little effort and an ounce of repentance. Such people have enemies where they could have had friends. In business, this can be lethal.

Try to prevent yourself from developing the sort of arrogance that makes it impossible for you or others to say, "I was wrong." Place the restoration of relationships above pride.

Questions for Reflection

Is there someone to whom you should communicate, "We're in this together"?

With whom in your life do you have a strained or broken relationship?

Is there any sense in which arrogance is preventing reconciliation?

To whom might you apologize—and for what?

GUIDELINE 28: One man wins success by his words; another gets his due reward by the work of his hands (12:14, NEB).

"Some people fix televisions. Others plow fields. Some manage pension plans. And some drive taxis." Different people make their livings in different ways and, so far, there does not seem to be much profundity in this proverb. However, I believe that the writer is hinting at something deeper, indeed, perhaps at several noteworthy ideas.

It is extremely important to find one's proper occupational niche. If one is best suited to fix computers, that is probably what one should do. If one is best suited to sell cars, that is probably what one should do. The software wizard who tries to sell Fords and the car salesman who tries to write programs may both be badly situated. After years of experience consulting for a high-level career guidance center, I became convinced that intelligent job selection is more than 50 percent of job success.

I am still amazed at how many people know almost nothing about their true career aptitudes and interests. They know, for example, that they "like working with machines" or that they are "good with budgets." But that is usually as far as it goes, if even that far. Often they drift into jobs to which they are poorly suited and which promise to bring them very little in the way of personal satisfaction.

People who do not know their own interests and abilities are often victims of the Peter Principle, which is that people tend to rise to the level of their incompetence. They continue to be promoted until they end up in a job that they cannot do well. There they often remain for years, doing poorly what they should never have been doing in the first place.

I once worked with someone who had always been brilliant doing a certain kind of job—so brilliant, in fact, that he got promoted to a much higher-paying position doing an entirely different kind of job. Almost all his energy was subsequently spent on trying to survive. The joy he once took in his work had been replaced by dread. He worried about getting fired and sensed that he was never going to be very effective at what he was doing.

He would marvel at others around him for whom everything seemed to come easy. To him, they seemed like naturals. The truth was that they would have fallen on their royal faces if they had tried to do his former job. Once installed in the new position, earning substantially more money than he did before, it may have made sense for him to continue in it. The emotional price of survival, however, turned out to be considerable, especially because he never did become any good at the job.

Because rewards in our society are not distributed evenly, most of us live under considerable pressure to move up. Many people are clawing their way to a top that they will never see and, even if they do, they may not enjoy it once they get there. Not everyone is cut out to be a chief executive officer or a board president. All of us have pockets of strength, regions of special ability and competence. The proverb writer is perhaps advising us to "play from our strengths" instead of our weaknesses. Perhaps the writer is also telling us that there are many noble ways to earn one's living. "Winning success by words" is not intrinsically superior to "winning success by the work of one's hands."

Evaluate your vocational assets and liabilities carefully, with ruthlessly candid humility. Do not let yourself be seduced by a few dollars into doing something for which you are ill-suited and which will never bring you fulfillment. If you have to decline a promotion to remain successful, do it!

Questions for Reflection

What are your best and worst job-related characteristics?

Are you doing what you should be doing?

Have you considered any kind of comprehensive career guidance?

Getting By with Integrity

GUIDELINE 29: Kings take pleasure in honest lips; they value a man who speaks the truth (16:13, NIV).

Whom can the board member count on to tell the truth about the corporation's financial position? To whom can the senior vice president in charge of sales turn for realistic projections? Where is the executive vice president who will tell the chief executive officer when things are beginning to fall apart? Sometimes it is the "king" who is the last to know that the walls of the kingdom are crumbling.

Near the end of the book of Genesis is the story of Joseph being sold into slavery by his brothers. Through a complicated series of events, Joseph eventually finds himself in Egypt, working in Pharaoh's court. Because of his integrity and competence, Joseph becomes a much-valued adviser to Pharaoh. In the end, because of his acquired power, Joseph helps the same brothers who, years earlier, had tried to ruin, if not destroy, him. Joseph's honesty with Pharaoh seems to have been a principal cause of his political ascendance.

People who wield great power, like ancient Egypt's imperial rulers, are forever being "rushed" by sycophants—those whose aim is to ingratiate themselves with the powerful. Like people with substantial wealth, whom can the powerful trust? Who can be counted on to tell them the truth? Whose integrity is guaranteed? "Will someone, anyone, tell me the truth?" This is what many heads of state, and many department heads and division managers, end up muttering to themselves.

A friend of mine once told me that, on the night he was appointed to public office, he heard from people that he hadn't heard from in years. Perhaps these people were calling out of pure motives. But how could my friend be sure that his callers were expressing genuine interest or congratulations? Or were they carefully crafting bits of verbal manipulation? For most of us, to be greatly concerned with such questions would be a sign of psychopathology. For the powerful, however, these kinds of questions become the ever-present cloud hanging over almost every human encounter. Prominent people live lonely lives. They are often surrounded by strangers only pretending to be friends.

Not only do the prominent have to worry about flattery; they also have to concern themselves with those who might betray their confidences. Anything they say can and likely will be used against them. As a White House budget director once found out, you never know when your friend and confidant is going to write you up in a magazine article. Integrity or the lack of it—the issue seems to jump out at you from every public quarter. On whose word can you rely? Always there are temptations to betrayal. Always there are risks.

Just about all persons, corporation presidents included, want two things that are sometimes contradictory. On the one hand, they want to hear the truth. On the other hand, they want to hear whatever will make them feel good at the moment. Thus the person who presumes to speak with a powerful person is always potentially caught between the jaws of these sometimes competing demands. To be of real value to a person in power, you have to be willing to sacrifice favor for candor. This is no small achievement, given that powerful people can hurt you. Short of such extreme punishments as termination, there is banishment down the hall, denial of promotion, curtailment of perks, lagging salary increases, and so on.

To minimize the risk of being punished for your truthfulness, you must use consummate tact. Say things gently, perhaps even tentatively: "Perhaps . . . maybe . . . you may . . . just a little . . ." Recall our earlier proverb about a king's threat being like a lion's roar. Nonetheless, people of integrity are in extremely high demand with the powerful. If you can establish yourself as such a person, you will very likely reap rich rewards for your troubles.

Not too many years ago, I came into some information that I strongly believed the chief executive officer of a particular company needed to hear. So, I called him up and made an appointment. I well remember the drive I made, through the pouring rain at the end of an already long day, to meet with him for only a few minutes. Those few minutes turned out to be crucial to our relationship because they allowed me to demonstrate that I cared more about him than playing it safe, since what I told him was potentially upsetting and offensive.

Questions for Reflection

Are you known to be trustworthy?

Do people see you as someone who will tell the truth, even at your peril?

Do you temper your candor with wisdom and tact?

GUIDELINE 30: He who rebukes a man will in the end gain more favor than he who has a flattering tongue (28:23, NIV).

Research indicates that friends expect, indeed desire, confrontation. While friendships are by nature supportive, they also serve as crucial forums for truth. "Only your best friends will tell you when . . ."

"John, let me say it straight. . . ."

"Joyce, look. No matter what you say, I have to tell you that. . . ."

"Ed, you can react any way you want to, but I'm going to say what I have to say, which is that. . . ."

John, Joyce, and Ed are three of my closest friends who would confront me just as quickly. Moreover, I might not expend this sort of energy or take these kinds of interpersonal risks for anyone other than a friend—unless, of course, it were my ethical duty.

It *is* our duty. All social organizations have unwritten norms for behavior, their informal codes of ethics. Part of our responsibility in the marketplace is to confront our associates, and even our customers, when it is in their best interests. I am well aware that such confrontation is rarely done if there is even the slightest risk that it might backfire. Nevertheless, it is usually our duty to do it.

The proverb goes even further. It suggests that, in the end, the person who takes the risk of confronting will be more favored than the person who slides into the formless ooze of flattery. No one respects a person who can say only "nice" things. If I have never heard you "say it straight," how can I trust you when you tell me how wonderful I am? But there is another reason that the person who "rebukes" wins more "favor."

It takes no genius to figure out that confrontation is risky. If you say something I don't like, I might get angry, write you off, renounce you for your insensitivity, and so on. Confronting me may mean either that you are too stupid to comprehend the risks involved or too obtuse to know that you'll hurt my feelings. Or you may be zapping me simply because you want to "get" somebody and I'm close at hand. But it could also mean that you *care* and are committed to me and my welfare. If I sense this sort of commitment from you, I am likely to make the same kind of commitment to you—as soon as I get over my irritation, hurt, or what have you.

Just about anyone can figure out that you have to be concerned to go out on a limb. To "take someone to task" (REB) is to take the high road, the hard road, the road fraught with hazards and difficulties. It is ever so much easier just to say nothing and "let everything pass." Having the courage and fortitude to confront another person in a loving manner, and with a loving intent, is strong evidence of virtue. Note that this is not to advocate chewing out people or ripping them to emotional shreds. It *is* to advocate, in the words of a best-selling book, "caring enough to confront."

A well-known football coach once said that the reason he drove his team so hard was that, by his doing so, his players would feel good about themselves regardless of how the season turned out. "If I'm soft on them, they'll always wonder if we could have won. If I pull everything out of them that they can give, there will be no wondering. We'll all know we did our best."

Our friends, associates, and subordinates want to know that they did their best. At the very least, they want to know that they had the means at their disposal to do their best, regardless of whether they chose to do it. Sometimes what they need, only we have: truth.

Take the risk of telling the truth, only do it graciously. Test the proverb writer's thesis that, in the long run, straight talk will win you more appreciation than flattery.

Questions for Reflection

To what extent do you flatter others?

Are there people you should confront and, if so, how can you do this most effectively?

GUIDELINE 31: A little, gained honestly, is better than great wealth gotten by dishonest means (16:8, TLB).
The upright find refuge in their honesty (14:32b, REB).

A popular myth, especially among those who are bitter about not having more money, is that money has nothing to do with happiness. This is plainly false. There is overwhelming evidence to suggest that money and happiness are positively correlated—but only at relatively low levels of income and, in the opinion of some experts, only until you get above the poverty level. Still, while having money may not, strictly speaking, cause happiness, it can help, provided that one's attitude toward money is wholesome and not pathological.

Money cannot, however, guarantee happiness or fulfillment. This is obvious if you stop to think about it for a moment. The richest person in the world, when faced by personal tragedy, hurts every bit as much as the poorest person in similar straits. So money may be a good thing, but it is not totally satisfying.

Money can be a source of a certain inner peace. It can, for example, provide you with freedom from economic worry. To be able to pay all your bills without hesitation is a comforting reality, while to worry about how you're going to make ends meet this week is not.

Treachery, however, tends to ruin peace. As a result, if you acquire money through devious means, this will almost surely destroy your sense of peace, since you will tend to pull yourself apart. Unless you are a total psychopath, a person without a conscience, you will not feel contented if you have come by your wealth dishonestly. Your guilt will get you. For a time, you may be able to forget the nature of what you have done, but sooner or later it will come back to haunt you.

Even if you can avoid being haunted by guilt, the fruits of your treachery may poison your life. You may have to pay back corrupt favors. You may have to withstand the hatred or scorn of those you wronged. You may even have to go to jail. The odds of achieving satisfaction by means of corruptly acquired wealth seem slim indeed.

As the second proverb suggests, honesty carries with it a certain inner security, a tranquillity of the soul. There is something tremendously reassuring about knowing that every penny you have has been earned honestly. Two thousand dollars earned with integrity may provide far more satisfaction than twenty thousand dollars acquired dishonestly. To some extent, the value of money is determined by the value you place on it. Money's worth is not established simply by the goods and services it will command. Part of the equation is how much you want these goods and services and how you feel about your own financial resources and the ways by which you have come into them.

Work hard. Save, little by little, and invest wisely. Eventually, you will probably prosper and enjoy some of the good things money can buy, including freedom from financial worry. Do not let yourself fall into the habit of getting your money in dishonest ways, or you will be potentially throwing away the very thing you are trying to acquire: satisfaction. Peace of mind is essential to satisfaction.

Questions for Reflection

To what extent, if any, are your ways of acquiring money compromised?

How might you fully achieve the inner peace that comes from honesty?

GUIDELINE 32: Charm is deceptive, and beauty is fleeting (31:30, NIV).

The writer is saying, in essence, that character is ultimately far more important and worthwhile than smooth skin, lean curves, or low cellulite—or, to turn things around, broad shoulders and rippled abs. Physical characteristics, however enjoyable, fade. No one with red blood denies the pleasurable aspects of physical beauty, which is exactly why this proverb was written. It is intended to get us to see the reality behind appearances.

Despite the effects of the various women's movements, inequalities still exist between men and women in the business world. Men in general remain more powerful. Many women still live in a kind of economic servitude to abusive spouses, and for complex reasons, most women are more marriageable when they are young. Men, by contrast, generally do not peak out in marriageability until their late forties or early fifties, and often later. Consequently, while a woman's marriageability still tends to decline with age, a man's increases.

Over time, this places the man in an ever more favorable position relative to the cold, hard marketplace. The proverb writer over two thousand years ago was sensitive to this inequity. The writer is telling men that they have no right to trade in their wives for newer models! To do this is to cheat the woman out of what is due her: praise, honor, respect, and recognition.

When you marry, you are making what is supposed to be a permanent commitment. This, at least, is what the words in marriage vows typically say. Although, as ethicist Lewis Smedes points out, marriage is better thought of as a covenant ("I will be something to you and you will be something to me") than a service agreement ("I'll do these things for you if you'll do these things for me"), the idea of a contract is sufficiently robust to remind us of what marriage is intended to be: binding.

I am not attempting to induce guilt in people who have been divorced, nor am I trying to make men feel bad who might have done some of the things we are considering. I am, however, highlighting the penetrating truth of "charm is a delusion and beauty fleeting" (NEB). A delusion is a firmly held bizarre belief. Today we might phrase the matter this way: sexual attractiveness can be deceptive; it is capable of enchanting you, to the point that you come to believe what is patently bizarre, namely, that it can satisfy the soul.

Some straight talk to men: You may find yourselves from time to time taken, perhaps enamored, with someone at the office or elsewhere. If so, don't be too hard on yourselves. You are human. If you have ideas of acting on your infatuations, be careful! I am writing at this moment not as an ethicist but as a psychologist who has seen much heartache and destruction come to both pack-the-suitcase-and-split men and left-on-the-doorstep women.

Straight talk to women: Almost any man who would become involved with you while you are married is a questionable risk. Do not be quick to run off with the power magnate, no matter what he promises you. And be faithful yourselves, because if you are not, the marriage will change even if your spouse never finds out.

Perhaps I am being too blunt. It's just that I've seen all that pain.

Questions for Reflection

Do you sufficiently honor those you should?

If and when you are tempted, do you count the costs of acting on your temptations?

GUIDELINE 33: A good man leaves an inheritance to his descendants (13:22, REB).

Life insurance that you take out on yourself is an investment whose "profits" you will, by definition, never live to enjoy. Purchasing such insurance, unless in the interests of gaining immediate economic or social advantage, is perhaps as close to pure altruism as many people ever come.

The impossibility of being the beneficiary of your own life insurance policy is perhaps why so many people do not buy one. While the reluctance of some may stem from a need to deny the inevitability of their own death or even the conviction that they can best protect their loved ones by investing in something other than insurance, some people just do not want to part with the premiums.

Any form of wealth that we set aside for the express purpose of bequeathing it to others represents something that we are giving away. The proverb writer is suggesting that this kind of giving is characteristic of a "good" person. Buying life insurance is, of course, only one way of building an estate.

As discussed in the first part of this book, society often rewards us for doing good things. Because saving and investing money are good for the economy, we are permitted to deduct certain kinds of earnings on our income tax return. Similarly, there are economic advantages connected with establishing certain kinds of inheritance vehicles, for example, trusts. Let us set such advantages aside, however, to consider some of the less obvious benefits of knowing that one will be "leaving an inheritance to one's descendants."

First, most of us have at least some ambivalence about making money. Although there is nothing wrong with money itself, the lust for money can cause us problems, and most of us realize this. Because we correctly sense that the quest for money can become a disease, some of us unconsciously avoid acquiring much of it. Nothing cures such self-sabotage like knowing that you want money for good reasons. Most, but not all, people agree that trying to accumulate money for the future benefit of loved ones is definitely a good reason! Imagine how unconflicted you would be about making money if you suddenly needed lots of it to save the life of a child.

Second, putting together some kind of inheritance for your dependents is a very direct expression of love. While many cynical people would debate this, love has a way of coming back to you. The giver is sometimes helped as much as, if not more than, the receiver. It seems to be built into the cosmos that goodness comes back to us. Most people have had the experience of profiting substantially from something that they did for others, without any view toward personal benefit.

Third, and most important of all, there is simply an inner peace in knowing that you are doing the right thing. Goodness is its own reward, certainly psychologically. You cannot be happy for long without peace.

While the question of just how much money you should leave to others is a highly personal one, there are good reasons for setting aside something for this purpose. I recommend that you do it as part of an overall program of integrity. Such integrity helps instead of hinders successful living.

Questions for Reflection

Do you work entirely for yourself, or do your goals include enhancing the welfare of others?

Are you systematically accumulating an inheritance to leave to your descendants?

Maturity and Judgment

GUIDELINE 34: To be patient shows intelligence; to overlook faults is a man's glory (19:11, NEB).
Patience heals discord (15:18b, REB).
The man in a hurry misses the way (19:2b, NEB).

When you live in the kind of fast-paced world that we do, it is not easy to be patient. If efficiency is not our god, it is certainly among our highest values. In just about every one of our endeavors, particularly in business, the idea is to get there first. Rush, run, race! This insane emphasis on speed tends to work against good judgment. It also tends to injure relationships. All three of these proverbs highlight an important aspect of patience,

Patience, to begin with, reflects a certain kind of social intelligence. Think of those persons in your life who, even though they may not have to be, are patient with you. Do they not strike you as wise? The "glory" of patience comes from seeing the bigger picture, from not being so petty that one gets hung up on the trivial. A patient person can move quickly, even rush intensely when necessary. The issue is how tolerant we are of others and of uncertainty.

Not only does patience help you get along well in the world, but it also helps you to help others get along well. Patience is reflected in an ability to hear their concerns. This, in turn, allows you to bring healing, which in business can make the difference between great success and terrible failure. If you have a talent for soothing hurt feelings, you carry with you the potential to salvage nearly lost accounts, almost breached contracts, and so on. Moreover, by not rushing in with superficial solutions or, worse, to express your own grievances, you give other people the time and mental space they need to work out their

121

problems, resolve their tensions, and settle their disagreements. As a rule, the further people get away from an upsetting event, and the more time that passes, the more they seem able to come to terms with what at first may have been totally unacceptable to them.

Finally, patience allows you to see the way instead of missing it. How many times have you searched frantically for something but, because you were in a hurry, you did not see it when it was right in front of you? Brilliance is sometimes the capacity to see the obvious. Yet nothing can be obvious if you do not take time to look. Let me show you how "obvious" something can be—once someone points it out to you.

What is it about a wheel that makes it such a clever invention or, to state the question differently, what makes a wheel a wheel? A wheel is not just something round. Egyptians used logs on which to roll huge blocks of stones, but such logs were not wheels. The answer is that a wheel has a fixed axle, that is, a cylinder that rotates about a shaft that is stably attached to a vehicle of some sort. Some civilizations used wheels to make toys, apparently without thinking to use them to do work.

What was the primary military value of the Great Wall of China, other than its function as a series of lookout posts that could quickly relay communications? If you count all of its branches, the Great Wall is close to four thousand miles long. It is ten feet wide at the base and, except for lookout posts, which are higher, it is thirty feet high. Warriors could use ladders to climb over the wall. And while it is always an advantage for an archer to shoot down, how many archers can you put on a wall? Horses were the tanks of the day, and a well-equipped mounted soldier was worth about thirty soldiers on the ground. The main military value of the Great Wall of China is that it helped prevent the Hun invaders, who relied heavily on cavalry, from conquering China.

Some of us are, by nature, more patient than others. Certain people move quickly while others move slowly. Some are high-strung while others are easygoing. Such traits are partly due to how our bodies are constructed, but they also relate to how we are put together psychologically and, indeed, to how we have trained ourselves. Within limits, you *can* alter your own "speeds." If you are impulsive, practice looking before you leap. If you are intolerant, practice tolerance. If you are high-strung, practice being mellow. Change may not come easily, but with dedicated effort it will come. Spend time every day imagining situations in which you tend to act impatiently, only visualize yourself being calm, slow, and circumspect.

Learning more patience will probably increase your social intelligence, your ability to help others, and your capacity to notice what others tend to miss because they are in such a hurry. Gaining control of your psychological speedometer will make you more likely to move at the right speed in whatever situation you find yourself.

Questions for Reflection

In which particular situations is it most difficult for you to be patient?

With which people are you the most impatient?

How might you develop more patience?

GUIDELINE 35: It is a trap for a man to dedicate something rashly and only later to consider his vows (20:25, NIV).

When I was teaching in a doctoral clinical training program, another psychologist once came to visit me and, while in my office, noticed that I had several copies of a book he very much wanted. The book was relatively expensive, and I had purposely acquired multiple copies so that, when it went out of print, as nearly all books do, I would be able to lend them to my students.

"Why don't you lend me one of these and I'll give you one back when it comes from the publisher?"

"Here," I replied, "just take one. Keep it. I have several."

I should have said, "No, I'd prefer to hold on to all of these," or even, "Okay, I'll lend you one if you promise to replace it."

What I did, in fact, was a classic example of what psychoanalysts call reaction formation, substituting in consciousness the antithesis of what one thinks unconsciously—for example, little boys and girls "hating" each other as soon as they begin to feel the stirrings of attraction to members of the other sex. I verbalized the opposite of what I really felt, only it happened so quickly that I scarcely had time to think about my own words. Later I grieved over the loss of the treasured volume.

The problem with what I did was that it was not from the heart. I was not a "cheerful giver." I did not have the inner love to follow through on my own offer.

Not all rashly given gifts or hastily made commitments are reaction formations. Often we genuinely intend to give the gift or make the promise, only we do not stop to count the cost. Later, when we realize the expense involved, we have second thoughts and occasionally deep regret. "What did I get myself into?" We "danced" to the joy of our own generosity, and now it is time to pay the piper.

The proverb is warning against poorly thought-out commitments. "Think through what you do before you do it. Don't offer, promise, or give what you do not want to, or what you will later resent."

Naturally, there are exceptions. If you find someone drenched in blood lying in the gutter, there is no merit in refusing to help simply because you might later "resent" it. Still, in the ordinary course of things, it is not good to offer what you cannot deliver willingly. All behaviors have consequences. The consequences of good behaviors sometimes have to be thought through just as much as the potential consequences of bad ones.

Resentment is an especially lethal emotion. It destroys friendships. It probably also causes heart attacks. Resentment tends to eat you up from the inside, thus seriously hindering your effectiveness. In addition, other people can usually tell when you resent them and your obligations to them, which is particularly insidious when you established these obligations through your own largesse.

Commit your time, energy, and belongings only after you engage in enough reflection to ensure that you will not later regret having made these commitments. Many of us tend to get in our own way. We become our own worst obstacles, sometimes by placing unnecessary constraints on ourselves. Carefully avoid creating "traps" for yourself by making impulsive commitments.

Questions for Reflection

Do you tend to commit too quickly?

Are there particular areas (e.g., time) where you are most vulnerable?

Are there particular people to whom you too readily make commitments?

GUIDELINE 36: A shrewd man sees trouble coming and lies low; the simple walk into it and pay the penalty (22:3, NEB).

A lemming is a small rodent that resembles a mouse. For complex reasons that relate to local overpopulation in their species, every three or four years hordes of European lemmings begin frantically to search for new territory. In their single-minded search, they ignore all obstacles. The lemmings inadvertently race toward high precipices, bound over them, and plunge to their deaths. This proverb warns us not to follow in the footsteps of the lemmings.

All of us have blind spots, areas of our lives in which we are vulnerable simply because we are insufficiently perceptive. Some people are easy marks for confidence artists. Others continually lose at corporate "hot potato," so that they get caught with the blame for mistakes and negligences not their own. Some people do not seem to notice when aggressions escalate and, as a result, become embroiled in senseless battles. Some habitually get involved with people who wrap them up in emotional flypaper, immensely complicating their lives with ridiculous hassles and misunderstandings. Some are "too good" for their own good: they help people who either do not want help or who repay kindness with malice.

As a psychotherapist, I had to learn to be prudent in how I expended my energies. Over the years, it became relatively easy to spot certain kinds of potential trouble and thus to avoid it. For example, I learned to sense when someone was likely to be financially unreliable (would not pay me for my hard work), excessively demanding (lots of unnecessary phone calls, paperwork, etc.), or chronically dissatisfied (no matter what I did, the person would probably complain). Learning to do this was not easy, and I am still getting better at "people reading." To the degree that I improve my vision, things go more smoothly for me.

In your business or profession, you may have to watch out for different kinds of things. For example, you may have to be very careful about what you say to some people, lest they betray your confidence, or you may need to be ever on the alert for the possibility of legal trouble. Every occupation has its hazards, which you can ignore only at great peril. Relatedly, every person has particular vulnerabilities, whether the tendency to trust too much or too little, to risk too much or too little, and so on. You may, for example, tend to hire people who are occupational time bombs or to ask the wrong people for help and advice.

Spending a few minutes each day with a pad and pencil will assist you to spot those things that are likely to cause you trouble. Routinely evaluate the pros and cons of your alternatives, as well as the strong and weak points of the individuals with whom you associate, especially those on whom you must rely. What potential troubles could ensue from the actions you contemplate taking? What do you have to watch out for with particular people? Such evaluations may seem cold and calculating.

You have to be willing to face reality to learn from it. If you truly want to do better in the future, admit to yourself where you have not done well in the past. Deliberately look for your own mistakes. I don't know about you, but I have made a lot of them. Keep in mind that old adage about how people who know nothing about history are doomed to repeat it. What is true of global history is perhaps even more applicable to individual history. Be astute in finding out which of life's punches most often nail you. When do you forget to duck?

Questions for Reflection

Looking back over your entire life, what sorts of dangers did you fail to see coming?

To what extent do you have a "lemming instinct"?

To what sorts of threats might you need to pay more attention?

GUIDELINE 37: Develop your business first before building your house (24:27, NLT).

This proverb is about fundamental economic priorities. While it certainly concerns money, by implication it also has to do with the wider spheres of time and energy. The writer is advising us to establish intelligent priorities and to stick to them. "First, solidly establish your source of income. Then, and only then, turn your attention to other things which, while fine in themselves, will only distract you from what ought to be your primary aim: solvency. Don't divert your energies into worrying about the house you live in (unless this relates to your earnings), where you're going to hang your favorite pictures, or whether the hedge is to be two or three feet high. Maintain your focus, your concentration, on developing your business."

The proverb is not exhorting us to neglect our loved ones or to become "work compulsives" who use their careers to run away from intimacy with people. Nor is it advising us to live in a shabbily decorated home. It is saying this: "Don't retreat from the hard business of making a living, into a fantasy world. Go out and cut it! Make your way. Do not be lazy or timid. Try to ensure the well-being of yourself and your family. Rather than lulling yourself to sleep by becoming soft or confused about your priorities, decide what you want and go after it."

From time to time I have realized that I have too much personal property in proportion to the size of my house, which has resulted in periodic de-junking. Our house is too small to hold all the "stuff." This, I think, reflects some sloppy priority-setting. It is not that I own anything terribly expensive, just that I own a lot of things that are not especially inexpensive. While I enjoy what I have—especially all those books—I think that I might have been wiser to save some of the money that I've spent on "things."

Few of us, of course, think and act with the rational efficiency of robots. We do much of what we do for emotionally toned reasons, some good, some bad, some wise, and some stupid. Because we are human beings and not collections of silicon chips, our motivations and thus our satisfactions can be exceedingly complex. We want this, because it is the right shade of blue, and not that, because it is the wrong shade of green. You cannot reduce your life to a software package or to a double-entry ledger without seriously tarnishing its existential luster.

Nevertheless, we have been given minds with which to think. To refuse to set down explicit priorities is to sentence yourself to live out implicit ones. It is a little like all that business about how not to make a decision is often to make one. This proverb contains guidance about how to make decisions—according to what will, in the long run, best establish the economic security of yourself and your family. Such advice does tend to generate some internal tension.

For years I wanted to write a particular novel. There was only one problem. Just about all first novels lose money, assuming that you can even get somebody to publish them in the first place. Many days I would have preferred to stay home and work on my novel but, instead, I trundled off to another consulting job. I did eventually complete it, but not at the price of putting my family in jeopardy.

Make sure you have a sensible plan for "developing your business" and distribute your resources according to it. Taking into consideration that there is never enough time to do everything one would like, keep your personal and your professional life in proper balance. There are always trade-offs and sacrifices. Life demands that we make choices. Love yourself enough to make them wisely.

Questions for Reflection

What do you want to accomplish in business this year and in the years ahead?

Are your energies distributed to maximize the probability that you will succeed?

Are you making the right sacrifices while refusing to make the wrong ones?

GUIDELINE 38: Like a madman shooting at random . . . is the man who deceives another and then says, "It was only a joke" (26:18, 19, REB).

Suppose you are walking along a city street, amid high-rise buildings and congested thoroughfares, and someone wearing a surveyor's hat asks you to hold one end of a blue string. "It will only take a few minutes," he insists. "My assistant is home sick today, and I badly need someone to help me with this measurement by holding this line tight." Or suppose you are driving through the same crowded city during the middle of a business day and round a busy corner, only to feel your front right wheel roll into a ditch.

Imagine, further, that after you faithfully hold the blue string for over fifteen minutes, your irritation ever mounting, you walk around the corner only to find another bewildered pedestrian holding onto the other end. Imagine also that, upon getting out of your car and determining that your front axle has cracked under the impact of the fall, all the while listening to the abuses of other motorists whose way you have blocked, you discover that the road has been dug up as a practical joke.

These are actual situations. At least once a busy New York street was dug up by impostors, and the "string sting" is, unfortunately, still exercised on people who, the next time they are asked to help, tend to do so with rather more reluctance.

Some people have what I can only take to be a perverse pleasure in playing "jokes" on others. Clinically, most practical jokers are acting out hostilities or bolstering their own sense of importance by victimizing others. The sickest part of the whole thing is when they say, "I was only kidding. Why are you getting so upset? It was just a joke." Most people who routinely play jokes on others want to be nasty without having to pay the price for their hostility. They expect to get away with imposing all kinds of discomforts on others under the guise of good-hearted humor. As psychoanalysts point out, however, there are no jokes. Although there are some jokes that are simply that and no more, beneath most jokes is some kind of serious statement or intention.

Does this mean we ought to go around with sour faces, unable to appreciate what is funny or to laugh at the genuinely absurd? Not at all. Wholesome humor does relieve tension and, at times, makes life more bearable.

It does mean that, if you are going to be hostile, you ought at least to admit to yourself and to others the nature of what you are doing. Mature people do not hide behind apologies or appeals to humor. If they get caught in some act of aggression or even in a deception, they are not so naive as to try to explain it away with a ridiculous claim such as, "I was only fooling." Such statements are primitive, if not pathetic, forms of what psychologists call "undoing." Undoing is the defense of trying magically to turn back the clock. It is an attempt to wriggle out of having to face the consequences of what we have done.

The proverb writer is making the strong statement that deceptions, especially when people try to cover them over with foolish excuses, can be deadly. More than one person has died because another person, who was the brunt of a "joke," turned out not to have much of a sense of humor. Similarly, more than one up-and-coming businessperson has been shunted off to Occupational Never-Never Land, or fired, because of an overdeveloped, if not marginally psychotic (psychosis is a form of mental disorder in which one cannot distinguish fantasy from reality), sense of humor.

Be careful about making jokes, especially since they tend to give away some of our baser impulses and instincts. Let others call to mind your maturity and good judgment long before they remember your funnies or your witticisms.

Questions for Reflection

Are you prone to making hostile comments or doing aggressive things and excusing them as jokes?

Are there people around you who are dangerous, and therefore ought to be avoided, because they like to victimize others with their "jokes"?

GUIDELINE 39: Argue your own case with your neighbour, but do not reveal another's secrets, or he will reproach you when he hears of it and your indiscretion will then be beyond recall (25:9–10, REB).

When I first arrived in Los Angeles many years ago, I was horrified by a psychotherapist who readily boasted about the movie stars he "had in therapy." Perhaps the stars did not mind. From time to time, it has been fashionable to have an "analyst." Nevertheless, this therapist was obviously quick to use the people he was no doubt sincerely trying to help in order to enhance his own reputation. Stars, after all, are people too. Like the rest of us, they hurt, they bleed, and they need privacy. Let me add that most therapists are extremely careful about honoring confidences. They would not betray a client if their fingernails were pulled out!

Even if you are not a psychotherapist, when someone gives you personal information, an implied contract is established. Just by listening, you are usually conveying the impression that you will treat what you hear as sensitive material. This implies, in turn, that you will not opportunistically use it for your own advantage. There are, of course, times when you should *not* allow such a confidence to develop and should therefore decline requests for confidential conversations. But if you agree to have one, you ought generally to honor its ground rules.

Let us assume, for the sake of illustration, that you get into a minor argument with one of your neighbors, say because he tends to accumulate unsightly piles of junk on his front lawn. Stan is clearly downgrading the neighborhood. When you ask him tactfully to remove some of the debris, he launches into a defensive speech. Your anxiety mounts and you become a little agitated. Finally, in exasperation, you say, "I'm not the only one on the block who is concerned about all this junk. Harry was saying the same thing just the other day."

Oops! Harry entrusted you with his private opinion, with which you have now gone public. Perhaps Stan will forget what you said. However, he may tell Harry. This could result in an awful mess, including the ruination of a long-standing friendship, all because of a few careless words. The courses of wars have been influenced by even fewer words,

Information takes on almost as high a value in the business world as it does in war. Corporations pay huge sums of money for certain kinds of information, ranging from the results of illegal industrial espionage to financial advisory services. Companies hire consultants. Wall Street buffs read the *Wall Street Journal*. IBM and other companies annually make billions of dollars by providing businesses with the means by which to store and digest information. The intelligence market is, indeed, big business.

It is sometimes tempting to use what one knows to get ahead, even if this means hurting someone else in the process. Good "corporate players," in fact, are often adroit at manipulating out of others confidential utterances. Fortunately, such information manipulators often become known for what they are, to the advantage of everyone else.

Watch what you say. You could easily make an inveterate enemy out of someone whose friendship you value but whose confidence you betray. Alliances, if they are to be more than fleeting associations of convenience, have to be built solidly on trust. You and the other person have to know that there will be no leaks, no down-the-river sales.

Questions for Reflection

Are you sufficiently careful about what you say?

Are you known as a person who respects confidences?

Are there certain people toward whom you should be on guard?

Are there people in whom you should confide nothing?

GUIDELINE 40: Don't visit your neighbors too often, or you will outwear your welcome (25:17, NLT).

Let's first consider the other side of the argument. Does familiarity ever breed not contempt but fondness?

A good deal of evidence now suggests that, in general, the more frequently people have contact, the more they like each other. Simple proximity—closeness—does seem to increase attraction and affection. Most of us, for example, long to visit the place where we were raised. We miss it as well as the people with whom we grew up.

It is interesting that some people stubbornly cling to certain manners of speech, for instance, the use of double negatives or slang words, not so much through force of habit but because such utterances psychologically signify to them what, and whom, they long ago came to love. We have strong preferences for the familiar.

Like most generalizations, however, the "proximity breeds liking" principle has to be qualified.

First, if people are obnoxious, being around them more is not going to endear them to us. If anything, it will make us like them even less.

Second, when proximity is combined with intense competition, people come not to love but to hate each other. Concentration camps provide some evidence for this, but more immediate proof comes from affluent suburbs inhabited by junior executives from the same company. Mutual character assassination is common in such socially competitive areas.

Third, like animals, only more so, human beings have a definite love for novelty, which is sometimes stronger than their love of the familiar. This is why toys become old so fast, to the emotional and economic dismay of the loving parents who bought them. Our quest for the novel is also the mainstay for the mass entertainment industries. While shows, films, and so on do sometimes provide us with aesthetically pleasing and educationally beneficial experiences, we probably value them most for their capacities to provide us with ever-new forms of stimulation.

Finally, people value their solitude. If God wanted us not to have any privacy, he would have given us mental telepathy, although I doubt that we could stand the strain! As John Steinbeck put it, we need to be together but we also need to be alone.

The author of this proverb is perhaps warning us against symbiosis. A symbiotic relationship is one in which two living organisms provide necessary services to each other. The plant and animal kingdoms are, at large, symbiotic when it comes to oxygen and carbon dioxide. Plants make oxygen and use carbon dioxide, while animals make carbon dioxide and use oxygen.

The problem with symbiotic relationships between human beings is that such arrangements tend to deprive the participants of their respective identities and freedoms. People ordinarily resent such deprivation, although they are often not conscious of exactly what it is that they resent. They just feel irritable or restless.

In a business environment, people are easily frightened by what, rightly or wrongly, they perceive as excessive dependence. Form alliances. Enjoy regular associations. Make friends. Only be careful that you do not crowd others too much, since what you may intend as warmth and camaraderie they may experience as suffocation. Absence does sometimes "make the heart grow fonder."

Questions for Reflection

Are you maintaining the right psychological distances with others, neither too close nor too far away?

Is there someone at this moment to whom you ought to grant more "psychological space," whether a superior, a subordinate, or a peer?

GUIDELINE 41: A fool betrays his annoyance at once; a clever person who is slighted conceals his feelings. An honest witness comes out with the truth, but the false one with deceit. Gossip is sharp as a sword, but the tongue of the wise brings healing (12:16–18, REB).

Although these proverbs concern the proper use of the tongue, a subject we explored earlier, I elected to discuss them here because they seem central to what we ordinarily mean by maturity. I want to emphasize the close connection between public speech and private wisdom.

First, an immature person reacts immediately when he or she is irritated. A mature person, by contrast, "stays calm" (NLT).

Second, an honest, and by implication a mature, speaker says what is true, while a dishonest one is "full of deceit." These statements were probably written to underscore the relationship between what we do and our reputations, and perhaps also between our hearts and our lips. People who routinely speak the truth are known for their honesty. For them, truth is a way of life.

Third, we can cut others with gossip, which always carries with it the potential to injure. Or, we can use our words to heal.

These proverbs exhort us to anticipate the effects of what we say. People are social beings as well as spiritual, psychological, political, economic, and physiological ones. All of us are susceptible to how others talk to and about us. Their words can soothe or inflame us, comfort or distress us, build up our reputations or tear them down.

Spontaneity, as much as its value is often touted, is not always a virtue. Too much spontaneity smacks of irresponsibility and plunges society into chaos. Violent criminals are excellent examples of overdeveloped spontaneity. Having never learned to limit how much they act in response to their momentary impulses, they simply do what they feel like doing, when they feel like doing it. Spontaneity, to be healthy, has to be balanced by control.

Take things easy when it comes to expressing displeasure or irritation. You can always do that. Once you lash out, however, it is hard to undo the effects of your actions. If someone angers you or hurts your feelings, let it ride for a while. Later, if you wish, you can launch into combat, but if you unthinkingly blurt out your reactions, things can quickly get out of hand and beyond your ability to regulate. Timing is all-important. There is a time to confront, and a time to hold off and plan exactly what you want to say.

These three sayings deal with the effects of public communication. How we make others look in public is an important determinant of how they feel about us. It is just not smart to put others in a position where they feel they must attack us in order to preserve their honor. "Blasting them" with your words, lying about them "on the stand" (to the boss), or gossiping about their frailties and indiscretions is certain to kindle their ire.

All this gets even more complicated when you consider that some people feel slighted when, in fact, no one has slighted them. While you cannot make yourself responsible for anyone else's "paranoid sensitivity," people with good social intelligence take into account the other person's level of "touchiness" before acting.

Practice "keeping cool," speaking only the truth, and resisting the temptation to be drawn into gossip. People will usually give you, or put you in charge of, their resources only if they trust you. They decide whether to trust you largely on the basis of your verbal behavior.

Questions for Reflection

Do you pause sufficiently before showing your ill humor?

Are you known for your mature honesty, so that others automatically trust what you say?

Do you use words to heal?

Avoiding Self-Destruction

GUIDELINE 42: The accomplice of a thief is his own enemy (29:24a, NIV). **Whoever sends a fool on an errand cuts his own leg off and displays the stump** (26:6, REB).
Don't associate with evil men (23:6, TLB).

We have all heard about "honor among thieves." There is none! People who steal from the customer or the company are just as likely to steal from you. To depend on the honor of a thief is to beg to be robbed.

A friend of mine put everything he had into developing a business with a person who, ultimately, turned out to be unsavory. My friend's business associate was anything but an overt thief, but when it came time to lock in the ownership of the company, the associate got greedy. As far as I know, my friend has yet to realize a dime for all his hard work.

As this illustration shows, accurate character assessment can be pivotal to success. Not all thieves are cat burglars who conveniently identify themselves by their black tights. Nor do potential embezzlers wear stripes across their chests in preparation for their new attire if convicted. Some are truly nice people who have only one or two episodes of larceny during their entire lives. Unfortunately, it only takes one such episode to ruin you, if you are its victim. So the first lesson in this three-proverb course in how to avoid self-ruin is to evaluate carefully the other person's R.O.T. ("rip-off tendency"). Among the best ways to do yourself in is to form a partnership, formal or otherwise, with someone whose R.O.T. is high.

Another way to hurt yourself is to choose a "fool" as your agent. Anyone who acts on your behalf with your permission is your agent, whether as assistant, messenger, accountant, attorney, seller, or buyer. Fools, almost by definition, muck things up. When a fool is acting as your agent, you are the person responsible for whatever mess ensues. Other people, noting the kind of representative you select, tend to conclude that it takes one to pick one. Protect yourself! Do not give the power to represent you to anyone who will not represent you well. Picking the right agent for the right job is far more important than selecting the right clothes to wear, and think of all the attention we give to that. If you choose your agents unwisely, you are, in the stark words of the proverb writer, "cutting off your own leg and displaying the stump."

The third proverb has been translated in several ways. "Do not go to dine with a miserly person" (REB) is one alternative, and another is "Eat not the bread of him who has a hard, grudging and envious eye, neither desire his dainty foods" (Amplified Bible).

When you consider the most prominent translations together, they seem to come out saying something like this: do not get involved with those who are unwilling. Few things in life are as offensive and demoralizing as pouring your life into someone who wants to give nothing back. The proverb writer is telling us not to get enmeshed with those who do not want to pull their own weight, economic or otherwise. Some people are determined always to make profit, to come out on top even with their friends. They part with their own resources grudgingly, as if they were thereby losing a contest, if not undergoing death. Involvements with such people can waste a great deal of your time and energy, since you will sometimes spend five hundred dollars to convince them to part with five.

Love yourself enough to stay away from the dishonest, to avoid the use of incompetent or otherwise unworthy agents, and to steer clear of those whose hearts are unwilling.

Questions for Reflection

While your work may force you to interact with dishonest people, can you spot them before you get entangled?

Do you choose your agents wisely, aware of how crucial such choices can be?

Do you avoid business involvements with those willing to give little or nothing?

GUIDELINE 43: Sometimes mere words are not enough—discipline is needed. For the words may not be heeded (29:19, TLB).
A net is spread in vain if any bird that flies can see it (1:17, REB).

Both of these proverbs have to do with the intelligent use of power.

How many times have you been in a store and overheard a parent say something like "Billy! I told you not to touch that." Billy touches it. Again the parent says, "Now, Billy. I told you not to touch things on the shelves." Of course, Billy continues to touch whatever he wants.

If the people under you have reason to believe that your words are empty, that you do not intend to back them up with consequences, they will probably ignore anything you say that they do not like. Sometimes they will become "passive-aggressive": "Oh, I forgot" or "Sure, I'll get to it, but I've been terribly busy." Other times they may become overtly rebellious: "I don't see why I have to do that" or even "Get somebody else to do it, because I will not!" I have seen senior executives neutralized by someone who simply said no. These executives just could not bring themselves to "take names and kick backsides."

Unfortunately, we are all given to occasional laziness and selfishness. One function of a manager is to limit the effects of such moral failings. This does not always have to be done with force, and indeed, punishment should be a last resort. However, unless you are so naturally influential that others eagerly comply with your every wish and whim, you will probably be seen as weak and unworthy of obedience if it looks like you are unwilling to use force when necessary. Others will simply think of you as afraid.

Although we do not like to admit it, much of what we do is governed by observable consequences. How long would you continue to work if you were not paid? How nice would you continue to be with your friends if they started abusing you? How much respect would you really show that superior you do not like if you could get away with saying everything you felt? Like it or not, the distribution and redistribution of resources drives much of society along. Your ability to manage people effectively is largely contingent on your ability wisely to grant or to withhold resources.

The second proverb is advising us not to make threats or announce our plans for invoking the powers at our disposal. Sometimes it is wise to telegraph such plans, in order to put others on notice. Often, however, it is wiser simply to act when the time is right, without prior warning.

A friend of mine was once appointed to an important job. When he moved into the offices supporting his new position, he inherited a career staff person who had seen appointees come and go. When my friend asked the senior staffer to do certain things, he got no results. He asked again, without effect. Wisely, he waited. Some time later, he had to complete a performance evaluation on the staff person, who had continued to ignore his orders and requests. The man came flying in.

"You can't do this. You'll ruin my career."

My friend opened his desk drawer and produced a list of everything he had asked the staff person to do. The latter instantly achieved enlightenment; they were able to work out an evaluation both could live with; and my friend never again worried about whether his instructions would be carried out. It is sometimes wise quietly to build your case.

Avoid the potential self-ruin that comes from failing to take necessary corrective action when it is required. Do not make empty threats. Indeed, consider not making threats at all. Just be sure that others know that you mean what you say.

Questions for Reflection

Do you sometimes talk when you should act?

Do you unwisely telegraph your moves before making them?

GUIDELINE 44: The wicked are caught in their own violence (21:7, NEB).
An evil man is brought down by his wickedness (14:32, NEB).
Never rob a helpless man because he is helpless, nor ill-treat a poor wretch in court (22:22, NEB).

Throughout most of this part, we have concentrated on the human consequences of prudent and imprudent actions. The principles we are now considering are among the most important in this entire book, because they have to do with what we might call "cosmic consequences." Evil tends to come back to haunt those who do it. It seems to operate like a boomerang. Hurl evil at someone and it is likely to fly right back at you and, perhaps, precipitate your undoing.

Can I prove this? Of course not. Do I believe it? Absolutely. Is this belief grounded in mere superstition? I don't think so.

Many stories have been told about people who do something heinous, only to end up on the shoals of personal tragedy. The newspapers and entertainment media are full of "bad guys finish first" stories. Other than hearing about the occasional murder of an underworld figure, most of us have little or no opportunity to observe the misery that malevolence characteristically brings to those who engage in it. Most of this misery is of the slow and insidious sort, unlikely to make it into the morning headlines.

The first proverb highlights what happens when people use violence to achieve their objectives. All of us have well-practiced strategies and tactics that we tend to rely on, especially under pressure. They are what I have called, elsewhere, our individual "default modes." Some people depend on congeniality to get their way. Others use persuasion. Still others are quick to give in, compromise, and yield to what others want in hopes of getting something for themselves in return, as a kind of sop.

Some of the more unsavory characters among us resort to force, whether in the form of subtle threats and modes of intimidation or in the form of blatant attack. An interesting but perhaps apocryphal story is told of the legendary industrialist and financier Andrew Carnegie, who, when another person wronged him, said simply, "I could sue you, but that would be expensive, so I think I'll destroy you instead." True or not, I find the story chilling. Yet most who live by the sword die by the sword. As the proverb suggests, they become ensnared in the web of their own violence.

Unscrupulous conduct of any kind functions as an insidious disease that, in the end, tends to consume the person behind it. That is the message of the second proverb. People who play with viruses end up infected. And unsavory actions provoke the wrath of others, which is another reason that malicious persons, sooner or later, often slip and fall on the banana peels of their own malice.

The third proverb starkly addresses the widespread but not very admirable human tendencies to become opportunistic when others are at a disadvantage, to abuse people who are without resources, and perhaps dismissively to lord it over those who are at or near the bottom of society. It is wrong to victimize the helpless or defenseless. Let me add that it is also imprudent, for you never know when the weak of today will become the strong of tomorrow.

Questions for Reflection

How much do you rely on aggression and violence to get your way?

Do you avoid violence, predation, and the appearance of evil?

Do you strive to do good, or have you become so jaded and cynical that you refuse even to try anymore?

Proper Priorities

GUIDELINE 45: Whoever relies on his wealth is riding for a fall (11:28a, REB).

Do not slave to get wealth (23:4a, REB).

Wealth is a tool. Money can provide us with purchasing power, the ability to obtain material things we want, as well as services that we need or enjoy, from getting someone to fix the shower to having someone build us a yacht. To become obsessed with money, however, is to confuse the means with the ends. It is to lose sight of the instrumental nature of money, that is, to let it become an end. Wealth can never properly be one's ultimate goal. To "slave after money" is to throw away your life in the pursuit of something that is best used to enhance the quality of the life one so foolishly throws away! To slave after money is a kind of idolatry. We tend to become servants, even slaves, of our idols.

Each of us has a "project of existence" to construct. Our experiences shape us, but we also shape our experiences. We make choices. We make interpretations of events. We have the power to determine, to a large extent, what we become. Success means creating an artful and godly existence. To take the mere accumulation of wealth as proof of success is to mistake a cartoon for a da Vinci.

These proverbs are telling us not to trust in wealth and not to wear ourselves out (NIV) striving for it. For what, then, should we strive?

We are, by nature, relational beings. Good relationships bring contentment and peace. Even if we lived alone on an island, we would carry on relationships inside our minds. We might even carry on audible conversations, perhaps suddenly to remember that we were physically alone. Surely we would carry on mental conversations. Wealth, properly used, is employed to enhance our relationships and our enjoyment of nature.

The most important "parts" of our world are people. The worlds of animals, plants, and so on are indeed beautiful, but their places are trivial in comparison with the world of human beings. The problem is not that some people love nature per se too much, but that they love it too much in relation to how much they love people. It is the same with money.

There are some very noble reasons for desiring money, as noted earlier. One good reason is that an accumulation of assets makes it unlikely that one will have to worry about whether one can shelter, feed, and clothe oneself and one's loved ones. Money can provide us with a certain kind of security. However, this kind of security is limited. It is freedom from inconvenience and petty hassle, but it is not necessarily freedom from loneliness or personal anguish.

The problem with compulsively pursuing money, aside from the adverse physical effects of working too hard, is that such pursuit distracts us from the truly important. Some compulsions (e.g., narcotics) and some distractions (e.g., looking at the scenery while driving) can prove fatal. Avarice is both a compulsion and a distraction that can be lethal to our psychological and spiritual health.

Do what you can to acquire wealth, but do not let the slave become the master and the master the slave. Every moment of your life is, essentially, a nonrenewable resource. Do not mortgage a present that comes only once for a future that may never come—a future that, even if it does come, is by nature incapable of replacing even one moment that has gone before it.

Money is a tool best used by those who know its limitations as well as its power.

Questions for Reflection

How much do you live each day in the belief that, if you only had more money, you would finally be secure?

Are you slaving so hard for wealth that the only thing you are likely to achieve is a massive coronary?

For what exactly do you want more money?

GUIDELINE 46: One who forgives an affront fosters friendship, but one who dwells on disputes will alienate a friend (17:9, NRSV).

Good relationships—those filled with candor, warmth, and intimacy—are the single best stress buffers we have. They are also what largely make life fulfilling. Without friends, we shrivel up and die emotionally and, in the end, become caricatures of what we might otherwise have been; we become mere shadows of humanity. The writer of this proverb is highlighting the importance of forgiveness to friendship.

Your friends will hurt you. Count on it. And you will hurt them. Get close to another person for very long and there is bound to be trouble or, in the words of the proverb, some kind of "affront." The question becomes what to do when you are the injured party.

What *not* to do is bury strong feelings. If the offense is minor, it is often best simply to ignore it. There's not much value in turning yourself into human flypaper, to which all manner of slight and innuendo, however small, clings forever, never to be released. If you find yourself stewing about something, however, it is usually best to bring it up because, as discussed in connection with Guideline 35, resentment is the enemy of all relationships.

Yet for any close relationship to survive, whether romantic or nonromantic, there will be times when those involved do not see eye to eye. No matter how much they talk about the problem or misunderstanding, whatever its nature, there will be no meeting of the minds. What does one do then?

Somehow—this is not always easy—you have to find a way to put it behind you. This does not mean that you repress it or deny your true feelings, which may range from pain to rage, but it does require that you find some way to let go of the issue emotionally. A lot of people have a terribly hard time doing this, and, frankly, I am one of them.

All human beings fall somewhere on a continuum, the ends of which have been labeled in a number of different ways. At one end of this continuum are the "sharpeners," "sensitizers," or "copers." These are the ones who make mountains out of molehills. Little issues become big ones because their emotional amplifiers are turned way up. At the other end of the continuum are the "levelers," "repressors," or "avoiders." These are the people who see molehills where there are mountains. Big issues become little ones because their emotional amplifiers are turned way down.

Few of us are at either end of this continuum; we fall between the extremes. Both orientations have advantages and disadvantages. Sharpeners are good at picking up nuances and they tend quickly to move into action, but they can also be touchy and overreactive. Levelers are good at remaining calm under pressure and look before they leap, but they can miss subtleties and be underreactive. As you have probably figured out, it is harder for sensitizers than levelers to let go of affronts.

If you are a sensitizer, you may have a tendency to dwell on (ruminate about) insults and injuries and, if so, it will sometimes prove difficult for you to get beyond them—no matter what the other person does. It would be irresponsible of me to try to provide you with a magic formula or quick gimmick for letting go because, in truth, there is none. The best thing to do is simply to recognize your own sensitizing tendencies, discuss this with the person who hurt you and, if you still find yourself unable to let go of the affront, talk it out with a third party, that is, someone other than the person you are unable to forgive. Just be wise in choosing this third party. The safest person with whom to talk, of course, is someone who is paid to listen, for example, a coach or counselor.

The most important thing here is to keep your priorities straight. Preserving a good relationship is worth almost any price you have to pay.

Questions for Reflection

Where do you fall on the continuum running from leveler to sharpener?

How hard is it for you to forgive affronts and put them behind you?

Are there friends or loved ones against whom you are harboring grievances?

Staying Out in Front

GUIDELINE 47: To learn, you must want to be taught (12:1a, TLB).
**Conceal your faults, and you will not prosper; confess and give them
up, and you will find mercy** (28:13, NEB).

Some years ago, when I was still working as a professor, a colleague came
into my office and said, "You know, I really respect you. You're not afraid to
put yourself on the line, to get right out there and take whatever comes, good
or bad. You send papers off to the best journals without fear of rejection, orga-
nize symposia with big names at national conventions, and write books before
you even have a contract. I wish I were more like that."

He looked sad and a little forlorn. I was grateful for the compliment, especially because he was a well-respected psychologist, but I also felt embarrassed. How do you respond to something like this?

The truly sad thing is that he was very gifted. On measures of sheer brainpower, he would have scored somewhere in the stratosphere, only he was hes-
itant to open himself up to criticism, to take the risk. He did not want to bear
the pain of someone telling him that he was not perfect.

I can identify with this because early in my life I was like that too. It actually took me a long time and a lot of injured feelings to learn that it is almost
always profitable to "put yourself on the line." If you do this often enough,
eventually it no longer bothers you—well, most of the time, anyway.

Truth is our friend—a hard lesson to remember when we can sense that
someone is about to rip us to shreds, perhaps with some justification. What we
are talking about here is taking the risk of discovering realities about ourselves
that, initially at least, we would just as soon *not know*. Even if we intellectually

understand the value of personal risk taking, we usually want to put off taking the risk if we are likely to get hurt. "I'll learn about myself later, maybe tomorrow. Right now, I don't want to deal with it." To learn, you usually have to want to learn. Sometimes wanting to learn may feel like wanting to suffer, and few of us want to do that.

Psychologically, it is extremely difficult to change something about yourself that you have not admitted. Until we come to terms with exactly what it is within ourselves that is causing trouble, it is almost impossible to get rid of such mechanisms of self-sabotage. This is because most of the self-destructive things we do, we do automatically, without much in the way of awareness. We do them, in other words, more or less unconsciously.

What the writer of the second proverb refers to as confession is closely related to what a psychoanalyst calls "free association," that is, saying everything without holding back. Obviously, you cannot go around all day confessing, but you can talk openly about yourself to a few trusted advisers.

Part of conventional business wisdom is that people who are effective know how to stonewall it and to finesse things. If you are stonewalling or finessing, you may be dangerously close to becoming an impostor. There is certainly a practical advantage to doing such things if you are swimming in a pool of hungry corporate sharks. Such is not the time to bleed—broadcast one's mistakes. There are times to admit one's errors and, in the words of another translation of "find mercy," to "get another chance" (TLB).

To refuse ever to discuss your own frailties with anyone is to guarantee that you will never learn very much about yourself. Not to benefit from such insight can be a major weakness, since ultimately what you are selling in business is you.

As much as you can, love correction. Using good judgment about where, when, and to whom to reveal yourself, "confess your faults," and, having done that, "give them up."

Questions for Reflection

How much do you truly believe that truth is your friend?

Do you love correction even when it gives you pain?

Are there people with whom you regularly share your faults and failures?

GUIDELINE 48: Walk with the wise and learn wisdom; mix with the stupid and come to harm (13:20, REB).
Never make friends with someone prone to anger, nor keep company with anyone hot-tempered; be careful not to learn his ways and find yourself caught in a trap (22:24–25, REB).

As human beings, we learn a great deal through imitation. We are incredibly adept at picking up the gestures, mannerisms, inflections, and so forth of those around us. The interesting thing is that such learning goes on automatically, without our having to think about it. People from Brooklyn talk a certain way, as do people from Texas. Children whose parents are in the New England social register talk and act differently from those whose parents are factory workers. People in the South usually have different attitudes from people in the North, and both have different attitudes from those in the West. Culture, high or low, is largely transmitted through the unconscious imitation of models.

To a considerable extent, we can control the kind of culture we internalize by carefully choosing our associates. If you want erudition, you probably ought to spend time with those who think and speak intellectually. If you want poise, you might consider spending time around those who move and speak with grace. If you want insight, associate with those who are insightful.

These proverbs tell us some straightforward things about how to exercise control over what we become. Associate with the wise and, lo and behold, become wise! Associate with the foolish, however, and you will only be misled. If you hang around with people who are volatile or violent, you will probably become like them and, as a result, find yourself "caught in a trap."

A considerable body of research has shown that, as a rule, teachers teach as they have been taught, not according to what all their education courses specify. Supervisors, on the whole, do with and to their subordinates exactly what *their* supervisors did with and to them, not what they were taught in business school or training seminars. Nearly everything we do is, of course, colored by a variety of influences, including formal education, films, books, and articles. The point remains, however, that perhaps the bulk of what we learn, especially our attitudes, comes through reflexive imitation. Whom we choose to associate with, and thus whom we destine (doom?) ourselves to imitate, is all the more important because attitudes, both stark and subtle, have a tremendous effect on how well we do in life.

Now, the trick in profiting from this guideline is somehow to convince yourself that none of us, including you, is immune from the powerful influences of models. We sometimes say to ourselves, "Well, other people may copy what they see and hear, but not me. It doesn't matter what I watch on television or what I read. Unlike a lot of other people, I think for myself."

The sobering truth is that all of us are far more influenced by what we absorb, especially from other people (models), than we usually realize. I do not know to what extent we are "part of all that we have met," but I do know that most of what we've met is part of us. You can resist any kind of social influence only so much. Beyond this—and there is much beyond our consciousness—we soak in our environments like sponges.

Select your influences, especially your companions, well. Do not let just anybody become your friend or associate. Spend time with those who embody whatever it is that you admire, people who—without either of you thinking about it—have something to teach you. Do not select people as your closest friends simply because they are like you. Choose those who can give you something worthwhile and, ideally, to whom you can give something of benefit in return. Those with whom you walk become your teachers.

Questions for Reflection

Do the people with whom you spend time demonstrate characteristics you admire?

Are there people in your life with whom you should spend less time?

Are there people with whom you should spend more time, so that you can learn from them?

GUIDELINE 49: Counsel in another's heart is like deep water, but a discerning person will draw it up (20:5, REB).

Most people are smart enough to know that when others ask for their opinions, they mostly want to hear praise and confirmation. People automatically, and correctly, translate "Say what you really think" into "Tell me what I want to hear." We have all learned the hard way, through such social punishments as neglect and disapproval, that to take such questions as "How am I doing?" at face value is often to invite trouble. So we make our translations and respond accordingly.

If you genuinely want to know what others think, you have to get behind their translation devices. Doing this ordinarily means convincing them that you are willing to endure pain, if necessary, to learn the truth. How does one do this?

First, do not ask people to tell you how you are doing when you are down and need affirmation. They will probably sense this need and, intelligently, provide you with support instead of with truth. However, if they actually miss the social cues and tell you something unpleasant, you will end up feeling terrible. Ask for truth only when you are in good enough psychological shape to hear it. When you need support, ask for that! Do not hunt tigers when you have only the strength to snare rabbits.

Second, ask specific questions. Think through what you want to know and frame your questions beforehand. You might even try writing them down. You can also ask people to rate you on a scale from one to ten with respect to various aspects of performance (e.g., warmth, sensitivity, effectiveness, assertiveness, expertise). Some people might even be willing to put some of this in writing for you. The nice thing about having a written document is that you can mull over it at your leisure, when your anxiety is low and you are not sitting face-to-face with the other person. Even if he or she does not want to write anything, you can always take a few notes, even on the back of a napkin. "That's helpful," you might say. "Let me jot it down."

Third, you can offer to exchange ratings and evaluations. This works best with people who are your peers or equals. You might say something like this: "John, I'd like to try something. Let me describe it, so you can decide if you're willing. Here are some questions. Maybe you could answer them about me, and I could do the same for you. Or, if you prefer, you can just answer them for me." Many people would be willing at least to do the latter.

These are some possible questions:

1. What do you see as my major strengths and assets?
2. What do you see as my major liabilities or limitations?
3. What are others' major criticisms of me?
4. What should I do or stop doing to become more effective?
5. What do you see me doing in five years, ten years, twenty years?

You may be able to come up with questions that work better for you, ones that address specific concerns you may have. These five questions will at least serve to get you started. Go easy at first. If you have not done this sort of thing before, you will probably find it a little frightening. So start with the easy questions.

Questions for Reflection

Is there someone with whom you might exchange constructive evaluations?

What questions about yourself would you most like answered?

GUIDELINE 50: To learn sense is true self-love; cherish discernment and make sure of success (19:8, NEB).

Love yourself! Please do not confuse this exhortation with the self-love talk that is bandied about on certain talk shows. Some of the most obnoxious people I have met are members of the navel-gazing set, devotees of the "self-esteem" cult with its "me first" ethos. The object of life is not only to love yourself. As discussed in the opening parts of this book, we also have a duty to love and take care of other people. Life is, in part, a school for goodness. Getting an A means becoming more loving and just.

The universe is intelligent! Life is very good at teaching us the difference between good and bad, if only we pause to listen to its messages. We need to come to see with cosmic eyes. To do this is, for us, to acquire sense. The

proverb writer tells us that by acquiring sense we will not only be loving ourselves, in the best possible sense, but also ensuring our success.

What, however, is success? We have already noted that success is far more
than money, which is a tool and, in our baser moments, the way we "keep
score." Let me close our last guideline discussion with a statement about what
I believe success includes.

To succeed is, in part, to discover and exercise our gifts and thus to do the
best we can with what we have; it is to face life with courage, committed to
learning such truths about ourselves as we can; success is to live with a pure
heart, wanting our own and others' good; and it is to be contented with what
we have, trying always to make life better for everyone.

It is perhaps insufficient to say that success is being everything we were
meant to be, since that leaves open the question of exactly what that is. Still,
I find it personally helpful to ask, "What am I supposed to be and do? What
is my life's mission?"

Being able to answer this question is perhaps the essence of "sense." Bear
in mind, however, that some of what we conclude in answer to these questions
may be nothing more than expectations that have been drummed into us by
others.

"Happy is [the person] who has found wisdom, and the [one] who has
acquired understanding; for wisdom is more profitable than silver, and the
gain she brings is better than gold" (3:13–14, NEB).

It is so much harder to quest after something intangible, such as sense, than
something we can see and touch, such as a new house, a better car, or a bigger television. Yet all the really important things in life—love, joy, peace, and
so on—are, by nature, intangible. To seek only what we can perceive with our
physical senses is, in the end, to have very little sense at all.

Go for it! "It" can stand for just about anything, from becoming president
to making millions. There is nothing wrong, and a good deal right, with success as it is conventionally defined. Just be careful that your definition of success is more enlightened and expanded than the traditional one, which
translates it only into dollar signs and status symbols. Seek the greater success
of living spiritually and "all these things will be added unto you."

Questions for Reflection

How do you define success—what does it mean to you personally?

When you get to the end of your life, what do you want to be able to say?

Summary

I want to take just a few moments to review some of the ancient advice contained in this part. Our purpose in examining these proverbs has been that they contain a wealth of practical wisdom. Because this wisdom centers on prudent versus imprudent conduct, it will go a long way toward helping us stay out of trouble, since imprudence is the soil in which unethical conduct grows best.

Here, in condensed form, is some of the practical counsel that we have considered:

> Words have tremendous impact. Use them to build friendships and to make others look as good as possible. Avoid conflict whenever you can. Listen carefully to the question before you answer it. Quietly, give well-chosen gifts, as long as giving them is neither illegal nor unethical. Pay your debts, both formal and informal, and treat others fairly. Do not hide your affection or appreciation; do everyone the favor of expressing it. Use your intelligence for noble purposes, so that others will admire and respect you. Develop patience and don't be impulsive. However, don't be afraid to take well-thought-out business risks. Recognize the power that other people have over you—don't ever underestimate it. Think carefully before choosing to rescue someone; make sure that person wants to be rescued before putting yourself at risk. Be equally cautious in choosing for whom you will countersign, whether what you are attaching your name to is a banknote or a special project. Whenever you can, suspend judgment until you know you have enough

data or evidence on which to base a sound evaluation or decision. Work hard because doing so still pays off. Attention to detail is often the road to achievement and advancement. Do as little as you can without fore-thought; plan thoroughly. Learn to conserve your resources, including but not limited to money, and invest as a way of life. Keep your speech appropriate to whatever is going on around you, and avoid chronic complaining. Don't overcommunicate and don't always say everything you're thinking; select what's best to say. Silence can be a great social asset. Share your wisdom and expertise only with those who genuinely want to hear it. Be modest rather than pretentious. Stay open-minded. Pay close attention to what others are trying to tell you, especially if you have power over them. Be on guard against pride and arrogance because they can engender massive resentment in others. We all have special gifts; discover what yours are and use them. Speak the truth; few things will hurt you as much as developing a reputation for slip-ping and sliding. Confrontation, however difficult, sometimes pays off in the long run, as long as you do it humanely and with the right motives, which should never be to injure. You are far more likely to be happy and contented in the long run if you build your life around hon-esty rather than deceit. Honor your loved ones by your loyalty—don't get seduced by youth and beauty, because these are declining assets. Overlook minor faults, especially in those close to you. Consider the consequences before you make any commitment. Be on the lookout for trouble and, as much as you can, avoid it. Develop your business before indulging your fancies and whims. Do not play practical jokes on others or use humor to excuse hostility. Honor the confidences of others; just be careful not to promise confidentiality when it would be unwise or improper to do so. Don't wear out your welcome—give other people their space. Speak graciously, truthfully, and without malice. Keep away from unsavory characters, sleazy associates, or incompetent agents. Back up what you say. Don't prey on the weak. Use whatever wealth you have for good, but do not place your trust in money or become its slave. Be open about your weaknesses and mistakes with people who will appreciate your openness. Actively, but prudently, ask other people for their evaluations, including any feedback they have on your performance. Spend time with those whose virtues you would like to acquire, especially those who are wise.

In Part 3, we will work our way through a number of ethical brainteasers, at least a few of which should prove challenging.

PART III

Testing Your Mettle

Try Your Hand at These

Challenging Exercises for the Ethically Conscientious

T his part contains a kind of self-administered examination consisting of two sections. The first contains thirty-five straight-forward, but not necessarily easy-to-answer, objective questions. These revolve around what I have called "simple ethical dilemmas" and, as such, have clear answers.

The second section presents eight more challenging problems, the kind that you might find at the end of a mathematics textbook. These problems revolve around what I have called "complex ethical dilemmas." Think through them, as best you can, before reading "Commentary on the Problems." You may find some of the eight relatively easy, but at least a few of them should give you a run for your money.

Try this one as a warm-up: A friend lends you a handgun, perhaps to use in target shooting, and a week later tells you that he or she intends to commit suicide and asks for the gun back. What should you do? We all know that not to return someone else's property is wrong. And yet, do you really want to return the firearm? (This problem, with minor variations, comes to us compliments of Socrates via his student Plato.)

Section 1: Thirty-five Questions on the Basics

Answer these questions as either "True" or "False."

1. Businesspeople who find themselves in ethical trouble nearly always see it coming.

2. Many people seem to believe that because they are intelligent and know the difference between right and wrong, additional education about ethics is a waste of time.

3. The kinds of ethical problems that prove most troublesome are *not* the relatively simple ones addressed in formal codes of conduct.

4. Executives have no higher level of responsibility to shareholders than nonmanagement employees.

5. It is unethical to mislead shareholders intentionally about the financial condition of a publicly traded company.

6. Accounting firms should be allowed to provide consulting services to companies whose financial statements they audit, as long as the annual reports of these companies openly state that this is occurring.

7. Most laws (e.g., criminal codes) specify what behaviors are not permitted and so, by implication, embody many of society's more important standards of good conduct.

8. Not all illegal acts are unethical.

9. All unethical business conduct is, by definition, also illegal.

10. The boundaries between "illegal" and "unethical" are sometimes fuzzy.

11. Fraud by definition involves the intent to misrepresent.

12. Lies of omission are rarely as harmful as lies of commission.

13. Many codes of conduct operate with what amounts to the force of law.

14. You can be imprisoned for certain kinds of unethical conduct, even if they are not illegal.

15. Citizens generally have an ethical responsibility to uphold the laws of their societies.

16. Any well-crafted set of ethical guidelines will tell you what to do when you face most complex ethical dilemmas.

17. As one ascends the ladder of almost any organization, pressures to compromise one's ethical standards generally increase.

18. Military personnel are not supposed to follow orders that are unlawful.

19. Some people are manipulated into doing unethical things by the threat of being labeled "not a team player."

20. Peremptory decision making usually proves useless when you are being pressured to sacrifice your integrity.

21. A person will never have to resign from a job if he or she tactfully insists on doing the right thing.

22. Whistle-blowers are almost always troublemakers and malcontents who lack loyalty.

23. Blowing the whistle on corporate wrongdoing should usually be a last resort.

24. If you file a formal report of corporate wrongdoing, it is prudent to consult a competent attorney but, in order to maintain your objectivity, only *after* you file it.
25. Few embezzlers believe that they merely took what the enterprise rightfully owed them.
26. Simple ethical dilemmas, as we have defined them, usually involve relatively straightforward issues of right versus wrong.
27. There is a close connection between simple ethical dilemmas and tragic moral choices.
28. An example of a complex ethical dilemma is having to choose between one's own welfare and the welfare of others when there is no law or other formal code of conduct to guide your actions.
29. When you face a troubling ethical dilemma, one of the best things to do is to consult others whose expertise and judgment you trust.
30. Certain chief executive officers (CEOs) are allowed by law to waive specific provisions of the Foreign Corrupt Practices Act.
31. Conflicts of interest are almost always easy to spot before they become problematic.
32. Avoiding conflicts of interest lies at the heart of many corporate and professional codes of conduct.
33. Falling into a conflict of interest rarely means taking on two potentially conflicting roles.
34. The law usually tolerates a public figure having conflicts of interest if he or she (*a*) openly declares them and (*b*) does not allow such conflicts to impair his or her objectivity.
35. Complex ethical dilemmas involve competing moral duties.

Answers with Explanations

1. False. They often fail to recognize potential trouble on the horizon.
2. True. Many people, to their detriment, believe that they need no additional training in ethics.
3. True. While people may agonize over simple ethical dilemmas, it is the complex ones that usually prove most troubling because there is often no way to know for sure what course of action is best.
4. False. Executives, like public accountants, have a special fiduciary duty to shareholders and, many would argue, also to employees, customers, communities, and society at large.
5. True. Regardless of how lawful or unlawful their actions, *anything* that misleads anyone about the financial condition of a publicly traded company is just plain wrong.

6. False. Stating such dual-role relationships in annual reports has nothing to do with it—an unacceptable conflict of interest remains.
7. True. With minor exceptions, laws codify what society takes to be right conduct by stating what may not be done without penalty (i.e., punishment).
8. True. While illegal acts committed in the course of doing business are unethical, illegal behavior outside the scope of business is not unethical in that context (although it may be unethical in other contexts); hence, running a red light is socially unethical, but in one's off hours it would rarely be construed as unethical business behavior.
9. False. You can do many unethical things that are not illegal.
10. True. Certain kinds of puffery, for example, are—to my mind at least—markedly unethical because they seem intended to mislead, but the law still allows them.
11. True. This, in fact, is the difference between misrepresentation and fraud.
12. False. Lies of omission can be just as bad, if not worse, than overt lies. If, for example, you fail to warn someone that he or she is about to fall from an unstable cliff headlong into the sea, it hardly improves your moral position to insist that you told no lies or even that you would gladly have warned the victim if only you'd been asked about local geological stability.
13. True. By violating formal codes of conduct you can, for example, lose your job or your right to practice a profession.
14. False. This is precisely the difference between unethical and illegal. You can do some egregious things and still not go to prison or even be compelled to pay a fine.
15. True. Philosophers differ in how far they go in insisting on this. While many ethicists agree that there is a point at which a citizen should break with specific rules of his or her society (e.g., when these rules grossly violate the dictates of conscience), it is commonly regarded as a basic civic duty to support the laws of one's society.
16. False. This is the pivotal difference between what we have called a simple versus a complex ethical dilemma. Codes of conduct often provide little help in resolving the latter.
17. True. For a variety of reasons, ethical decisions typically become harder, not easier, as one acquires more power and responsibility.
18. True. This is a major provision of the Uniform Code of Military Justice.
19. True. Being branded as "not a team player" can be a powerfully coercive device, one that is all too commonly used to pressure employees into doing things they know to be wrong.
20. False. This is precisely when peremptory decision making is likely to

prove *most* helpful. There will always be the sometimes slippery issue of what, precisely, will and will not compromise one's integrity. When the silent alarm bells inside your head begin to ring, it is at least time to pause: when in doubt, don't.

21. False. This unfortunately is simply not true, even for the most tactful among us. There is sometimes a price to be paid for integrity, and this price can include leaving a much-valued job or organization. The "good guys and gals" do not always win, but at least they avoid letting others turn them into scoundrels.

22. False. While some whistle-blowers are chronically unhappy and inclined to cause trouble, many are people of strong moral conviction and deep loyalties.

23. True. All other avenues should usually be exhausted before taking this relatively drastic step—unless, of course, what you are troubled about poses an imminent danger and is thus distinctly time sensitive.

24. False. The time to consult an attorney, if at all possible, is *before* you blow the whistle, in part because such consultation may affect the manner in which you do so; you may also have overlooked less extreme alternatives that a good lawyer might spot immediately.

25. False. Most embezzlers seem to believe that they simply made off with money that was owed them, sometimes as compensation for ill treatment or lack of promotion.

26. True. While a person may struggle mightily in the face of temptation, the issue of right versus wrong is relatively straightforward. This is because, with simple ethical dilemmas, a formal code prescribes what ought and ought not to be done.

27. False. The close connection is between complex ethical dilemmas and tragic moral choices.

28. True. This is a common type of complex ethical dilemma.

29. True. Consulting those whose competence and judgment you trust is nearly always a good idea, and the sooner, the better.

30. False. This is an important point to understand, not just in relation to this specific law but when it comes to any law. No executive has the right to "waive" any provision of the law; he or she is not "above the law" and cannot put you above it either.

31. False. As discussed earlier, sometimes they are exceedingly difficult to spot.

32. True. This is a tremendously important principle to grasp, because ignorance of it has caused incalculable heartache and pain to countless people throughout the ages. For this reason, it lies at the heart of many business and professional codes.

33. False. This is precisely what it *does* mean. With each role comes a set of duties and expectations. When two or more sets of such duties and expectations exist, the door is wide open for them to collide—and often they do.

34. False. No! Openly declaring a conflict does absolutely nothing for a public figure, except perhaps to make him or her seem oblivious to a crucially important principle of ethics. And as stated earlier, the law presumes that no one is superhuman enough to maintain his or her objectivity when such a conflict exists.

35. True. This, in fact, is the definition of a complex ethical or moral dilemma—one in which you are torn in at least two mutually exclusive directions, and you cannot avoid making a decision.

Section 2: Ethical Brainteasers

1. You are a civil engineer who has worked for fifteen years in the Chicago office of a national construction firm—one of just a few—that specializes in urban transportation. Your spouse does not work outside the home; you have three children in college who count on you for regular and substantial financial support; and, you are not independently wealthy. In fact, you and your spouse often struggle to make ends meet. Your professional expertise lies in helping to design bridges and tunnels for rapid transit systems and because of your depth of experience and excellent track record, you are widely regarded within the firm as the most competent person to do such work. The executive in charge of the firm's San Diego office has asked that you be assigned to him for the next two years because a new subway and light-rail network is to be built there and the firm has won the lucrative contract. When you arrive in San Diego, having sold your home in Illinois, you discover that your new boss has definite ideas about how much earthquake protection should be designed into public transportation structures in Southern California, and it is clear that his standards for safety are distinctly lower than yours. A forceful person, he says that he expects you to adopt his standards, since they meet or exceed what is required by code and doing so will save the firm considerable money. You have concluded that if you push too hard for what he regards as "gold-plated earthquake protections," you will be fired. The job market has been tight for some time, and no one is predicting a fast turnaround. To whom do you owe duties, and what are they?

2. You work for a tyrannical take-no-prisoners supervisor who, in her words, "does not suffer fools gladly." She has been known to terminate

employees on the spot for "inadequate performance." This volatile boss also has clearly identified favorites—"pets"—who have impressed her with their high-quality work. Some of your coworkers have told you, off to the side, that you seem to be among her favorites—to be a member of what they, perhaps enviously, call her "Star Chamber." A week ago, she told you that she wanted to hear a presentation on new approaches to customer service. Sincerely wanting to help a younger subordinate advance in the company, you invite him to make the presentation rather than seizing this opportunity for yourself; if the presentation goes well, he will be a "star." Based on instructions you provide, your subordinate works all week, late into the night, preparing his talk on the company's innovative approaches to serving customers, for example, allowing customer service representatives more power and discretion in responding to complaints. The presentation, however, is a disaster because it turns out that your boss wanted to hear about what other companies were doing: "I already know about *our* customer service—why are you wasting my time?" Clearly, you misunderstood what she wanted and, based on this misunderstanding, inadvertently injured the very person you were attempting to help. You also need to keep your job and to begin to think of ways that you can make it up to the subordinate in the future. What is the primary ethical issue? Are lies of omission as ethically questionable as lies of commission?

3. You are a junior executive in a company that has promised to raise $100,000 for a worthy charity, expecting that the money would come from corporate "friends," such as wealthy members of the board of directors. Donations have been disappointing, totaling only $42,000, and the senior vice president of finance has asked you to call your "vendors" and request that each contribute at least $3,000. She implies that bringing in donations will demonstrate your "commitment to the team" and that this, in turn, is likely to advance your career. What is the key ethical issue here?

4. A coworker who is not getting along with her boss asks to speak with you in confidence. You agree to meet her for a quick cup of coffee after work, and she informs you that she is about to turn in her letter of resignation and, further, that she is thinking about "going to the newspapers" with some "very nasty information." You probe for additional facts and she tells you that her boss, who is in charge of purchasing supplies for the entire corporation, has been accepting free vacations, some of them in Europe, from an outside vendor. Because you believe strongly in the mission of your company, which manufactures critically

important pharmaceuticals and gives many of them away in great quantities to third-world countries, you persuade her not to "go public" with this because, first, it would injure the company's reputation for rock-solid integrity and, second, such a disclosure might diminish its continued ability to acquire much-needed government funding. Politicians from another state, which houses the corporate headquarters of a rival corporation, have been aggressively gunning for your enterprise in hopes of securing more federal support for their state's pharmaceuticals firm; they would no doubt salivate at the mere thought of sinking their teeth into the raw meat of such a scandal. You also urge the woman to inform senior management about what her boss has been doing or at least to release you from your promise of confidentiality so that you can do so. Regardless of how much you implore her, she says no, adding that a potential future employer might want to call her present boss, whom she does not want to antagonize. She also insists, with considerable passion, that she does not want to get branded as a "whistle-blower." She resigns and, for years, you are haunted by the knowledge you have, all the while suspecting that the complimentary vacations are still going on. How would you analyze the wisdom of what you have done or failed to do? Is it defensible to violate your ex-coworker's confidence? Is it defensible not to inform your employer? How does the duty to honor another person's confidence compare with the duty to protect the assets and integrity of the company for which you work—which should count more heavily? Is there a clear "right answer" here, and if so what is it?

5. You work for a nasty and malicious boss who has ruined more than a few careers and, in one instance, probably precipitated the suicide of a depressed employee by mercilessly humiliating him. He has also been known to engage in sexual harassment. The boss loathes you and, although you do your best to hide it and respond to him in a civil manner, you thoroughly despise him for the way he treats people. Two angry female employees accuse him of making sexual advances, behavior toward which your company is especially intolerant because of two recent lawsuits that proved costly. An investigation ensues, and it appears that your abusive boss is about to be terminated. In your opinion, it couldn't happen to a nicer guy. In a moment of anticipatory triumph, the two women confide in you that they "made the whole thing up," clearly expecting you to congratulate them for their cleverness and to delight in the reality that "the predator has finally been turned into the prey." And you do. He deserves it, if anyone does. What ethical considerations come to mind?

6. A fellow employee has been fired, unjustly in your opinion, and as a result has had his identification badge confiscated. He is forbidden, therefore, to enter the premises of your company, which does sensitive work for the government. The terminated employee suddenly appears in the doorway of your office. Looking frightened and seemingly out of breath, he informs you that he has returned, briefly, to say good-bye—they gave him no chance to do that properly—and to pick up some personal effects that, in haste, he left behind, such as his walnut desk set and a cherished picture of his children. You hear heavy footsteps coming from down the hall, around the corner. The man dives under your desk to hide, and your boss appears, asking if you've seen the terrified man. If you say yes and turn him in, the man whose knees you can faintly hear knocking will surely be arrested. He will be unlikely ever again to obtain a security clearance, which almost guarantees that he will be unable to find work in his specialty. What do you do and why? What are your duties?

7. You are under considerable financial strain because your mother needs a major operation and has no medical insurance. While delivering some documents to a senior officer of your company, you overhear a conversation about how it is about to be acquired by a larger corporation and that the stock price of your company is likely to "go up by at least $12 a share, maybe more," as soon as the news breaks in a day or two. Your mother's surgery is going to cost somewhere in the vicinity of $40,000, and you have only $4,000 in savings and other liquid assets. You reason that if you buy three thousand shares of your company's stock when Wall Street opens in the morning, you may be able to sell them in a few days and acquire the money you need. What are the issues here?

8. Your company has introduced a new benefits option, according to which employees will be able to choose between their current health plan and an alternative that, you have been told, promises to save the company millions of dollars each year. Both plans are complex and difficult to understand, but you have it on good authority that the new alternative is clearly inferior. Your boss expects you aggressively to promote the new plan, to persuade your subordinates to switch. He tells you that your performance appraisal will be based in part on the "conversion rate" (percentage who change plans) for the 102 people who work under you. Moreover, you are in line for a major promotion. Your daughter has been accepted to Harvard, Yale, and Stanford but, without this promotion and the salary increase that comes with it, you will not have the money to send her, even with educational loans. What ethical duties stand in tension here? What duties do you owe and to whom?

Commentary on the Problems

Problem 1. You have duties to your employer, your spouse, your children, the society, and finally to yourself. Let's consider them in that order. You owe your employer the duty of doing what it, as a company, wants, and this is most clearly expressed in the form of what you are told to do by your supervisor. You could, of course, "appeal" the disagreement to senior executives in the firm's national headquarters and, under the circumstances, this may be the best thing to do. But in the end, you have the duty to do what "they" want you to do, as long as it does not break the law or violate your conscience, and therein lies the problem—it does violate your conscience. Note, in passing, that while you have a fifteen-year investment in the company, it in turn has a fifteen-year investment in you, which may strengthen the duty. Your duty to your spouse is probably based on the implicit contract (agreement) that the two of you have crafted by virtue of the way you have chosen to live: you work outside the home while she doesn't. It is reasonable for her to expect that you will continue to support her, especially after she has uprooted her life to move to California. Your duties to your children are similar. They may have chosen the colleges they did on the assumption, which may amount to an implied promise, that you would fund all or a substantial part of their education. Even if they didn't, you have been funding it, and they have a reasonable expectation that you will continue to do so. Your duty to society is more ambiguous and difficult to specify. To what extent it is your duty to get your company to build to standards above code depends, I suppose, on what your technical knowledge and expertise suggest to you about the adequacy of this code. If it is painfully lax, you have a much higher duty than if it is relatively stringent. And in the end, the assessment of lax versus stringent is going to be a matter of personal judgment—yours, in this instance. Finally, we come to your duty to yourself. If this comes down to a matter of personal integrity—if it passes neither the sleep nor the newspaper test—you may elect to resign, a decision that appears as if it might prove costly, given the job market. There is no pat answer.

Problem 2. The major ethical decision here is whether or not to own up to the fact that your subordinate missed the mark as a direct result of what you told him. Your musings about how you can "make it up" to him seem, to me at least, to amount to little more than rationalizations and what psychoanalysts call the defense mechanism of "undoing"—trying, through actions such as apologies, to make it as if whatever it is you're trying to undo never happened. But it did, and you were the cause of it. The fact that you need your job, I would submit, is largely irrelevant to the nature of your duty, which is to inform your take-no-prisoners supervisor, head of the Star Chamber, of your role in what happened. There is, of course, the issue of when to do this, for example, whether to stand right up in the meeting as soon as her displeasure surfaces or to wait until a more opportune time. This might be a time to rely on that gyroscope we discussed in Chapter 5. Waiting, however, may not be the best idea, since the longer you put it off, the more agony both you and your subordinate are going to have to endure. One consideration in this case is that if you do not own up, your subordinate may tell your supervisor anyway; it is always better to confess your sins than to have someone else do it for you. But that, in my view, should not be the motivating force behind your decision. It should be to rectify the injury that you inflicted, albeit unintentionally, on his career. As far as lies of omission, they can be every bit as terrible as lies of commission, depending on the circumstance, and sometimes worse. Neither lies of commission nor of omission are inherently any worse than the other, although it must be said that most people mistakenly assume that lies of commission are automatically more grievous.

Problem 3. The problem here is abuse of power. Vendors, especially if they are small companies, are especially vulnerable to such pressure. Although some large vendors have internal rules in place that prohibit them from making such donations, precisely to avoid their having to deal with the kinds of pressures portrayed in this case, it would be a trivial matter for them to provide $3,000. A small vendor, by contrast, especially one with few clients, has less power to resist such pressure. Moreover, more pain would be inflicted on a small vendor. Not long ago, a case just like this in Northern California made it into the papers, to the embarrassment of the company putting on the squeeze.

Problem 4. This is another tough problem, particularly because of the government funding, an issue to which we will return presently. You probably made a mistake in agreeing to confidentiality in the first place. It might have been better to state, as soon as you could, that if your coworker were to inform you of ethical misconduct by others, you would have no choice but to report it. This might have shut off the flow of information, but perhaps to do so would have been better than your having to carry it around in silent misery for years. Companies that accept government grants are under more stringent guidelines and more scrutiny than those that do not, and for this reason, your duty as a citizen to disclose the information may override your duty to honor the confidence. If you were a psychologist or a member of the clergy this might not be the case, since people bring strong expectations of confidentiality to relationships with such professionals. If you were to choose to reveal the information, the best way to do it would be discreetly, to someone in authority within the company whose judgment you trust.

Problem 5. This problem is similar to Example 4.8, in which as a police officer you have to decide whether or not to go along with a plot to frame a criminal. Do the ends justify the means? People with ethical sophistication might well recommend against such dishonesty, even for such a worthy cause as getting this obnoxious fellow fired. Assuming that you elect not to participate, the real ethical issue may become whether or not to tell on the two women who "made the whole thing up." After all, you work for a guy who has repeatedly demeaned women, a person who is described in the case as "nasty and malicious" and as having "ruined more than a few careers." Would I betray what, I am sure, they considered to be their confidence in talking with me in order to save this slimeball? I really don't know. It would be a hard decision.

Problem 6. You have to turn him in, and quickly. If you and other employees have to hold security clearances, on the face of it that, in my view, makes clear your course of action. No matter what the frightened man says or what you think about the fairness of his termination, you would probably turn yourself into a criminal if you harbored him, pure and simple. You have no duty whatsoever to help him deceive those who are looking for him, and this would be so even if no security clearances were involved. You might feel a human duty to be kind to him, but that would certainly not mandate turning yourself into a shield for his illegal activities. His sentimental reasons for trespassing—and violating the security protocols—are irrelevant.

Problem 7. If you use the information to buy and sell stock and get caught, you will go to jail. Companies have extremely sophisticated ways of monitoring the purchase and sale of such securities by persons connected in any way with them. I have seen more than one person "go up the river" for this sort of thing. Notice that in this case I did not ask about your ethical duties to your mother, because they are largely if not entirely irrelevant. You could argue that using the information to make trades is in principle no different from stealing bread to feed a hungry family. And as in stealing bread, you would act on such reasoning only at great peril. If you ended up wearing striped clothes, who would take care of your mother?

Problem 8. This problem is similar to the one in Problem 3 because it involves a potential abuse of power. But obtaining a good conversion rate probably also requires you to act as if you think the new medical plan is better. You have a duty to strive for the good of your company, and in this case it appears that a high conversion rate will save it "millions of dollars each year." And yet lying—which is what this comes down to—is not something most of us would be proud to do. Think once more of the sleep and newspaper tests. Let me add that it matters little, if at all, that your daughter is ready to go to a wonderful college and that you need the promotion and the extra money. Embezzlers often say that they needed the money. I would argue that you shouldn't do it—but that's only my opinion. To close this discussion on a lighter note, I want to relate the story about the man in the tiny company whose president wanted to switch to a new benefits plan, only to do so he had to have all employees sign up. Within a few days everyone in the place had signed, except for one lone holdout. His fellow employees strongly encouraged him to go along with the change, and his supervisor first urged and then hollered at him, all without success. Finally, the president summoned the man and said, "If you don't sign this, Manfred, you're fired!" The man took out his fountain pen and promptly wrote his name on the document. When he left the president's office, the other employees, eager to find out if Manfred had stuck to his guns, asked what happened. "I signed," he said cavalierly. "Why did you change your mind?" they asked in astonishment. "Because," he said, "the president explained it. I never understood before." Indeed, he had not.

Ethics is the disciplined study of responsibility and, in the end, ethical decisions force upon us this question: Can I live with this action? They also raise another question: What kind of person do I truly want to be?

Recommended Readings

Books of General Interest

Badaracco, Joseph L. Jr. *Defining Moments: When Managers Must Choose between Right and Right*. Boston: Harvard Business School Press, 1997.

> Written by a professor of ethics at the Harvard Business School and a former Rhodes scholar, this volume focuses on what I have called, in my book, complex ethical dilemmas. While I do not agree with everything Badaracco writes (e.g., "truth is a process"), his book has value in its realistic exploration of the sorts of ethical problems executives, managers, and supervisors face every day—problems to which there are few, if any, pat answers.

Bennett, William J., ed. *The Book of Virtue: A Treasury of Great Moral Stories*. New York: Simon & Schuster, 1993.

> This compilation, with commentary by a prominent public figure, contains writings illustrative of moral dilemmas and noble choices. It was followed two years later by *The Moral Compass: Stories for a Life's Journey* (New York: Simon & Schuster, 1995), which is also worth time and attention.

Coles, Robert. *Lives of Moral Leadership*. New York: Random House, 2000.

> Coles has spent much of his life studying moral development. In this book, he focuses on some well-known leaders, such as Mahatma Gandhi; others who are relatively obscure, such as community organizer Danilo Dulci; and still others who are fictional, such as a character out of one of Joseph Conrad's novels.

Greenleaf, Robert K. *Servant Leadership: A Journey into the Nature of Legitimate Power and Greatness*. New York: Paulist Press, 1977.

> This book contains the major essays written by a man who, until his death, was among the most important thinkers of the twentieth century. His writings continue to be influential in business circles and beyond. Readers who are inspired by the simple elegance of Greenleaf's message may also want to peruse the Spears volume (see below).

167

Peck, M. Scott. *A World Waiting to Be Born: Civility Rediscovered.* New York: Bantam Books, 1993.

> The contents of this book, written by a psychiatrist and one of America's best-selling authors, are closely related to the material contained in *Street-Smart Ethics.* Peck's writings nicely combine the theoretical and the practical. Readers who appreciate the value of basic civility may also want to explore Stephen L. Carter's book, *Integrity* (New York: Basic Books, 1996). Peck's earlier *People of the Lie* (New York: Simon & Schuster, 1983) is also relevant and thought-provoking.

Spears, Larry C., ed. *Reflections on Leadership: How Robert K. Greenleaf's Theory of Servant-Leadership Influenced Today's Top Management Thinkers.* New York: John Wiley & Sons, 1995.

Books for the Academically Minded

Kaplan, Robert D. *Warrior Politics: Why Leadership Demands a Pagan Ethos.* New York: Random House, 2002.

> I list this well-written and provocative work not because I necessarily endorse its message—which is worth serious reflection—but because it is an important contribution to the contemporary literature about the moral issues surrounding war. The book has been something of a best-seller at American armed-service academies. A correspondent for the *Atlantic Monthly,* Kaplan also received considerable attention for his earlier and equally engaging book, *The Coming Anarchy* (New York: Random House, 2000).

Nussbaum, Martha C. *The Fragility of Goodness: Luck and Ethics in Greek Tragedy and Philosophy.* Cambridge: Cambridge University Press, 1986. Rev. ed., 2001.

> This formidable volume, written by a professor of Law and Ethics at the University of Chicago, treats the writings of Aeschylus, Aristotle, and other important Greek thinkers. Not for the intellectually faint-hearted, her book includes detailed treatments of such classics as Sophocles' *Antigone,* which is used as discussion material in academic courses on leadership and business ethics,° and Plato's *Republic.*

Simmons, A. John. *Moral Principles and Political Obligations.* Princeton, N.J.: Princeton University Press, 1979.

> This book explores the complex and often subtle relationships that surround political duties, for example, to obey the laws of the land. Special attention is paid to such contemporary thinkers as Herbert Hart, John Rawls, and Robert Nozick.

°As reported to me by Harold G. Buchanan, Professor Emeritus Robert K. McKersie of MIT's Sloan School of Management treats it in his course "Choice Points: Readings on the Exercise of Power and Responsibility," which "draws extensively from the set of readings [used] by former dean Abe Siegel." The course, which "has been in existence for many decades," centers largely on "classic drama and fiction" and, in addition to Sophocles' work, treats Shakespeare's *Julius Caesar,* Robert Bolt's *Man for All Seasons,* Mary Shelley's *Frankenstein,* Michael Frayn's *Copenhagen,* Franz Kafka's *Penal Colony,* Joseph Conrad's *Secret Sharer,* Herman Melville's *Billy Budd,* Arthur Miller's *Death of a Salesman,* Henrik Ibsen's *A Doll's House,* Antoine de St. Exupery's *Night Flight,* Ha Jin's *Waiting,* and—finally—Niccolò Machiavelli's *The Prince.*

Rawls, John. *Lectures on the History of Moral Philosophy.* Edited by Barbara Herman. Cambridge, Mass.: Harvard University Press, 2000.

The editor of this book states, "There is little doubt that modern political philosophy was transformed in 1971 with the publication of John Rawls's *A Theory of Justice*." Admittedly "heavy reading," this volume is based on lectures Rawls delivered in a course he taught at Harvard. It begins with an introduction to "Modern Moral Philosophy (1600–1800)," then moves on to explore, in this order, the contributions of Hume, Leibniz, Kant, and Hegel.

Index

About the Author

A nationally recognized psychologist, speaker, and seminar leader, Clinton McLemore has consulted for over twenty-five Fortune 500 companies. The author of four previous books, his many professional articles have appeared in the prestigious *American Psychologist* and other scholarly journals. His ideas have been featured in such publications as *Securities Industry Daily*, *Today's Leader*, and the preeminent *Harvard Business Review*. Dr. McLemore is president of Relational Dynamics, Inc. (*www.relationaldynamics.com*), which specializes in executive coaching, team building, and the development of advanced leadership development tools, such as "360s," organizational surveys, meeting-effectiveness measures, and upward evaluation methods. His company also conducts workshops on life planning and on business/professional ethics.